DATE DUE

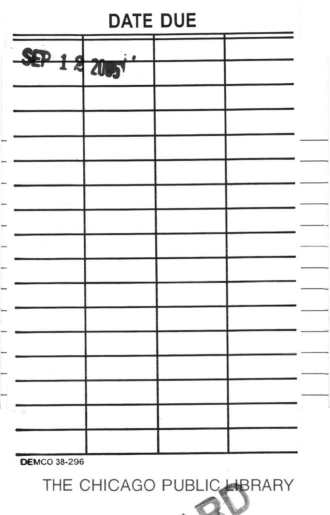

The Constitution

Other titles in *The Constitution:*

The First Amendment
Freedom of Speech, Religion, and the Press
ISBN: 0-89490-897-9

The Second Amendment
The Right to Own Guns
ISBN:0-89490-925-8

The Fourth Amendment
Search and Seizure
ISBN: 0-89490-924-X

The Fifth Amendment
The Right to Remain Silent
ISBN: 0-89490-894-4

The Thirteenth Amendment
Ending Slavery
ISBN: 0-89490-923-1

The Fifteenth Amendment
African-American Men's Right to Vote
ISBN: 0-7660-1033-3

The Eighteenth and Twenty-First Amendments
Alcohol—Prohibition and Repeal
ISBN: 0-89490-926-6

The Nineteenth Amendment
Women's Right to Vote
ISBN: 0-89490-922-3

The Constitution

The Preamble and the Articles

Daniel Weidner, Ed. D.

Enslow Publishers, Inc.

40 Industrial Road   PO Box 38
Box 398   Aldershot
Berkeley Heights, NJ 07922   Hants GU12 6BP
USA   UK

http://www.enslow.com

Dedicated to: Elisabeth, for so much enthusiasm, Megan Winter for the idea, and those who would learn from it.

Copyright © 2002 by Daniel Weidner, Ed. D.

Library of Congress Cataloging-in-Publication Data

Weidner, Daniel W.
    The Constitution : the preamble and the articles / Daniel Weidner.
       p. cm. — (The Constitution)
    Summary: Explores the preamble and individual articles of the United States Constitution, as well as how this important document was written, how it has developed through the years, and how it is enforced.
    Includes bibliographical references and index.
    ISBN 0-7660-1906-3
    1. Constitutional law—United States—Juvenile literature.
    2. Constitutions—United States—Juvenile literature.
    [1. Constitutional law. 2. Constitutional history.
    3. Constitutions—United States.]
    I. Title. II. Series.
    KF4550.Z9W45 2002
    342.73'02—dc21   2002008163

Printed in the United States of America

10 9 8 7 6 5 4 3 2

Illustration Credits: Collection of the Supreme Court of the United States, p. 98; Corel Corporation, pp. 25, 109; Library of Congress, pp. 14, 65, 68, 88, 92, 114, 125; National Archives, pp. 9, 48, 58, 75, 77, 122; Reproduced from the *Dictionary of American Portraits,* Published by Dover Publications, Inc. in 1967, pp. 50, 79, 90, 100, 119.

Cover Illustration: National Archives

Contents

Introduction

On December 13, 1952, two aging handwritten documents were placed in helium-filled cases, enclosed in wooden crates, laid on mattresses in an armored Marine Corps personnel carrier. They were escorted by troops, two tanks, and four servicemen carrying submachine guns down Pennsylvania and Constitution avenues to the National Archives. The papers that had been stored in a half dozen secured vaults over two centuries would now reside on permanent display in this Washington D.C. museum.

There are few things or people in the United States who can enjoy the kind of care and respect those documents received. But there are few documents as vital to Americans and perhaps the world as the Declaration of Independence and the American Constitution.

Since that day in 1952, millions of American and foreign visitors have filed through the National Archives past the glass cases that help preserve and display these most important documents. Together the Declaration and the Constitution represent the struggle for independence and freedom from tyranny that meant so much to America's earliest citizens. But the Constitution is much more than mere symbolism.

The words the Framers of the Constitution penned on four pages more than two centuries ago are as alive and vibrant today as they were the day they were written. For over 200 years law makers have followed its dictates. Still, the meaning of each phrase within the Constitution is often a source of arduous debate. Whether to interpret the document loosely or strictly is a constant question. That debate was just part of what the Constitution's Framers may have expected and wanted.

The first vision of an American Constitution came with the victory over the British in the American Revolution. Victory had cost the Americans a great deal and with the war behind them they were left to determine how to pay their debts and how to govern themselves. The Articles of Confederation was their only guide and it did not do enough to protect the rights of Americans. Instead the United States was fast becoming a land of thirteen isolated states. With a weak national government, the states were on the brink of economic disaster.

To address this, in the summer of 1787, a group of prominent Americans (at least thirty-four were lawyers) from twelve of the thirteen existing states (Rhode Island sent no representatives) met in Philadelphia, Pennsylvania. In addition to lawyers there were soldiers, planters, educators, ministers, physicians, financiers, and merchants. The states represented were Connecticut, Delaware, Georgia, Maryland, Massachusetts, New Hampshire, New

Jersey, New York, North and South Carolina, Pennsylvania, and Virginia.

The Framers came to Philadelphia by horseback, stagecoach, private carriage, and boat. Many were late. Because the delegations from only two states were at first present, the members adjourned from day to day until they achieved a quorum of seven states on May 25. Seventy-four delegates were appointed to the convention, of which 55 actually attended sessions.

The group assembled in the Long Room of the Pennsylvania State House—the same room where the Declaration of Independence had been signed a decade before. They worked in secrecy with windows and doors closed to ensure no eavesdroppers heard their discussions. Freshly-spread dirt covered the

This painting by John Froelich depicts the adoption of the U.S. Constitution at Independence Hall, Philadelphia, Sept 17, 1789. George Washington, presiding, is standing at the right.

cobblestone street in front of the Pennsylvania State House, protecting the men inside from the sound of passing carriages and carts. Guards stood at the entrances to ensure that the curious were kept at a distance.

Meanwhile, inside, the Framers began discussing their hopes of bringing states together with a central government that worked for the states' common good. Their motivations varied. Among the chief points at issue were how much power to allow the central government, how many representatives in Congress to allow each state, and how these representatives should be elected—directly by the people or by the state legislators. All agreed the Articles of Confederation was not meeting the needs of the states and a stronger, more cohesive national government was needed. Many worried about granting too much power to the federal government. Others insisted a strong central government was essential. Few agreed on whether the Articles of Confederation should remain intact with a few amendments or if a sweeping new document was needed. Serious conflicts arose at the outset, especially between those representing the small and large states.

Over the course of nearly four months, these men put together what would become one of the most important documents in history—the United States Constitution.

The Constitution's 4,500 words outline a new form of government with some similarities to England's Magna Carta and some new concepts never before applied to a federal government. The Constitution describes a government with three main branches: the Executive or presidential Branch, the Legislative Branch (House of Representatives and Senate), and the Judicial Branch. Each branch works both independently and in conjunction with the others and no branch has supreme power. The Constitution was signed by thirty-nine of the fifty-five delegates on September 17, 1787. Three months later Delaware became the first state to ratify or accept the Constitution. New Hampshire became the ninth state to ratify the document and the Constitution went into effect on June 21, 1788.

The Constitution had been very unpopular with some delegates. They felt it still allowed tyranny within the government. A list of amendments amounting to a bill of rights, was recommended. By the fall of 1788, Framer James Madison had been convinced that not only was a bill of rights necessary to ensure acceptance of the Constitution but that it would have positive effects.

Madison's support of the Bill of Rights was critical. One of the new representatives from Virginia to the First Federal Congress, as established by the new Constitution, he worked tirelessly to persuade the House to enact amendments. By December 15, 1791, three-fourths of the states had ratified the ten amendments now so familiar to Americans as the Bill of Rights.

Since that time seventeen more amendments have been added, including one to repeal another. They reflect the changes of the American people and their needs. The Fifteenth Amendment allowed African Americans to vote. The Nineteenth Amendment did the same for women. Most importantly, perhaps, the Bill of Rights has remained the primary model for judicial actions.

The main origins of the completed Constitution lie in centuries of experience in government, the lessons of which were brought over from England. They were further developed through the practices of over a century-and-a-half in the colonies and early state governments, and in the struggles of the Continental Congress. Its roots are deep in the past; but its endurance continues. All national constitutions that followed the American one show its influence; it has been copied extensively throughout the world.

The American Constitution has its limitations. It does not give American people their rights and liberties—it only guarantees them. The people had all their rights and liberties before they made the Constitution. The Constitution was formed, among other purposes, to make the people's liberties secure— not only against foreign attack but against oppression by their own government. The Framers set specific limits upon their national government and upon the States, and the result is a treasured example of cooperation and compromise.

The Preamble to the United States Constitution

1

> We the People of the United States, in Order to form a more perfect Union, establish Justice, insure domestic Tranquility, provide for the common defense, promote the general Welfare, and secure the Blessings of Liberty to ourselves and our Posterity, do ordain and establish this Constitution for the United States of America.
>
> —Preamble to the United States Constitution

After the American Revolution ended in 1783, the new United States lived under rules set by a document called the Articles of Confederation. The Articles did little more than create a loose alliance among the thirteen original states. There was no real effort to create a strong national government.

Most Americans at the time were afraid of the government. They remembered all too well the treatment they had endured under British rule. They were determined to prevent the same from happening in their new country.

But the Articles of Confederation quickly proved unable to handle the many problems of the new nation. Having just fought a long and expensive war, the states and their citizens were in deep debt. Under the Articles of Confederation, the Congress had no power to make laws relating to money. It could not even demand that the states pay their share of the taxes needed to run the government. The Congress had no way to enact programs that might help make people's lives better.

As a result, many people became dissatisfied with the government. They had fought a dangerous war in the hope of making freer, more prosperous lives for themselves and their families. Now, as people faced unbearable debt and saw that the government was powerless to help them, that dream seemed impossible.

Few Americans at the time had any real sense of being part of a nation, so most took their frustrations out on their state governments. In Massachusetts, for example, a large group of farmers faced losing their property because of their debt. They attacked the local arsenal in an attempted uprising in 1786–1787. They were frustrated with the government's refusal, or inability, to help their situation.

Known as Shays' Rebellion, this incident showed just how desperate things had become. It was time to create a new

The violent uprising of disgruntled farmers known as Shays' Rebellion made clear the need for a strong government to ease financial burdens.

Constitution to help end the many problems caused by the Revolutionary War.

In the summer of 1787, a group of prominent, well-educated Americans from every state (except Rhode Island, which did not send any representatives) met in Philadelphia, Pennsylvania. Over the course of a few months, these men put together what would become one of the most important documents in history—the United States Constitution. It would come to be considered a shining example of an effective democratic system of government of the people, by the people, and for the people.

The Preamble states the six general purposes of the Constitution.

The first of these was "to form a more perfect Union." While of course something cannot be made "more perfect" the Framers wanted to bind the states together more closely by creating national laws and courts. They hoped each state would feel it was part of a nation rather than an independent political unit.

The second purpose was to "establish Justice." The Articles of Confederation did not provide for federal, (or national), courts. The only way to carry out the law was in the state courts, none of which conformed to any particular nationwide standard. Nor did any state court have authority to decide cases that involved national issues. The new Constitution would provide for establishing a United States Supreme Court as well as a system of national courts.

The third purpose of the Constitution was to "insure domestic tranquility."

The country was extremely uneasy during the period from the end of the American Revolution to first President George Washington's inauguration in 1789.

The Framers wanted to be sure that there would be national peace.

The Framers also intended to "provide for the common defense." Under the Articles of Confederation, Congress could not raise an army, no matter how urgently the country might need protection. The Constitution would give the federal government the power to raise military forces to defend the nation and enforce federal laws.

The Constitution's fifth purpose was to "promote the general Welfare."

This statement expressed the Framers' desire to help make a better life for the people by encouraging trade.

Lastly, the Preamble referred to the Framers' intention to "secure the Blessings of Liberty." These men knew that national strength could help protect liberty or freedom for the people.

The preamble is not, strictly speaking, a part of the Constitution. Rather, it explains the reason for the Constitution and its purposes. It follows the principle set out in the Declaration of Independence: that governments get "their just Powers from the Consent of the Governed."[1]

In 1789, however, the phrase "We the People" did not mean all the people. It referred only to the minority who had political rights (about one adult white male in six). Over time, however, the Constitution was amended. Today, the government set forth in the seven Articles of the Constitution of the United States applies to nearly all American adults.

2

The Legislative Branch, Article 1, Sections 1–3

The Legislative Branch

Section 1. All legislative powers herein granted shall be vested in a Congress of the United States, which shall consist of a Senate and House of Representatives.

The House Of Representatives

Section 2. The House of Representatives shall be composed of members chosen every second year by the people of the several states, and the electors in each state shall have the qualifications requisite for electors of the most numerous branch of the state legislature.

No person shall be a Representative who shall not have attained to the age of twenty five years, and been seven years a citizen of the United States, and who shall not, when elected, be an inhabitant of that state in which he shall be chosen.

Representatives and direct taxes shall be apportioned among the several states which may be included within this union, according to their respective numbers, which shall be determined by adding to the whole number of free persons, including those bound to service for a term of years, and excluding Indians not taxed, three fifths of all other Persons. The actual Enumeration shall be made within three years after the first meeting of the Congress of the United States, and within every subsequent term of ten years, in such manner as they shall by law direct. The number of Representatives shall not exceed one for every thirty thousand, but each state shall have at least one Representative; and until such enumeration shall be made, the state of New Hampshire shall be entitled to choose three, Massachusetts eight, Rhode Island and Providence Plantations one, Connecticut five, New York six, New Jersey four, Pennsylvania eight, Delaware one, Maryland six, Virginia ten, North Carolina five, South Carolina five, and Georgia three.

When vacancies happen in the Representation from any state, the executive authority thereof shall issue writs of election to fill such vacancies.

The House of Representatives shall choose their speaker and other officers; and shall have the sole power of impeachment.

The Senate

Section 3. The Senate of the United States shall be composed of two Senators from each state, chosen by the legislature thereof, for six years; and each Senator shall have one vote.

Immediately after they shall be assembled in consequence of the first election, they shall be divided as equally as may be into three classes. The seats of the Senators of the first class shall be vacated at the expiration of the second year, of the second class at the expiration of the fourth year, and the third class at the expiration of the sixth year, so that one third may be chosen every second year; and if vacancies happen by resignation, or otherwise, during the recess of the legislature of any state, the executive thereof may make temporary appointments until the next meeting of the legislature, which shall then fill such vacancies.

No person shall be a Senator who shall not have attained to the age of thirty years, and been nine years a citizen of the United States and who shall not, when elected, be an inhabitant of that state for which he shall be chosen.

The Vice President of the United States shall be President of the Senate, but shall have no vote, unless they be equally divided.

The Senate shall choose their other officers, and also a President pro tempore, in the absence of the Vice President, or when he shall exercise the office of President of the United States.

The Senate shall have the sole power to try all impeachments. When sitting for that purpose, they shall be on oath or affirmation. When the President of the United States is tried, the Chief Justice shall preside: And no person shall be convicted without the concurrence of two thirds of the members present.

Judgment in cases of impeachment shall not extend further than to removal from office, and disqualification to hold and enjoy any office of honor, trust or profit under the United States: but the party convicted shall nevertheless be liable and subject to indictment, trial, judgment and punishment, according to law.

Section 1: Creating Congress

The Founding Fathers created Congress (the legislature) to carry out legislative, or law-making, functions.

The Congress makes laws through powers written in the Constitution. Any powers not clearly granted or that cannot be "reasonably" implied (suggested) from those granted are denied, and are kept for the states. The power of Congress is very broad. There is little it may not do, as long as it does not violate specific constitutional or individual rights.

The "Powers" of Congress are named in the fifty-three paragraphs, or items, of Article I of the Constitution (covered in Chapters 2-5 of this book). No one may use these powers except the two branches of Congress—the Senate and the House of Representatives.

Section 1: The Bicameral Congress

Under the Articles of Confederation, Congress was made up of one house, and each state had one vote. The larger states (large in population, not geographic size) were unhappy with this plan. They felt representatives should be distributed according to each state's population with one representative elected for a certain number of people. The larger a state's population, the more representatives it would have. The Framers of the Constitution agreed to a compromise. Congress would be bicameral (consisting of two houses): the House of Representatives and the Senate.

The members of the House of Representatives were to be chosen according to the population of the state. This plan satisfied the larger states. On the other hand, each state was to have two representatives in the Senate. This assured the small states they would not be overpowered by the large states.

The basic ideas of the men at the Constitutional Convention came from the English Parliamentary system: the House of Representatives (in England, the

House of Commons) would reflect the attitudes of the ordinary people, whereas the Senate, like the British House of Lords, would reflect the views of the upper-class.

The Framers believed that the existence of two houses would prevent legislation from being passed too hastily. The Senate and House have practically equal powers of legislation.

Section 2: House of Representatives

Members of the House of Representatives are called congressmen or congresswomen, or representatives. They are elected for a term of two years.

The Great Compromise included a provision: senators would be chosen by state legislatures while representatives of the House were to be elected directly by the people of each state.

In 1963, the Supreme Court, in the case of *Wesberry* v. *Sanders*, held that a state legislature is also required to establish congressional districts. As nearly as possible, each of these must hold an equal number of people. The Court stated, "one man's vote in a congressional election is to be worth as much as another's."[1]

Since that time, the Court has come to use "the one-person, one-vote principle." The concept is that, when a state legislature creates congressional districts, it must justify any change by showing that it tried to create the districts as nearly equal as possible.

Section 2: Qualifications of Representatives

The Constitution lays out the qualifications a person must have to be elected as a representative. There are three.

First, a representative must live in the state he or she

will represent, but not necessarily in the district to be represented. Representatives almost always, however, do live in the district that elects them. Most Americans feel that representatives should be closely acquainted with the needs of their districts.

The second qualification states that a representative must be at least twenty-five years old, while the third is they be an American citizen for at least seven years.

Section 2: House Membership and Direct Taxes

When the Constitution was written, the Framers knew they would have to compromise if they hoped to create a workable government. The number of representatives in the House and Senate was one of the great compromises. Representation in the House of Representatives (as well as the levying or placing of direct taxes) is divided among the states according to the number of people each has.

Section 2: Slavery and the Constitution

In the years after the American Revolution, many states held slaves, especially in the south. In distributing representatives and placing taxes, the question arose: How should the slaves be counted? The word *slave* was not used in the Constitution until the amendments. Slaves were simply called "other Persons."

The Northern states, where there were few slaves, were perfectly willing to have slaves counted when taxes were being laid, since Southerners would have to pay more. The North, however, proved unwilling to have slaves counted when it came to assigning representatives for the House. White people of the South felt just the reverse—slaves were fine to count when adding representatives, but should not count for tax purposes.

The "Three-fifths Compromise" was designed to settle the issue. This compromise is often called the "Federal Ratio." It stated that every five slaves would be counted as three free people when determining both taxes and congressional representation.

The Constitution excluded American Indians from taxation, however. This provision no longer holds completely true. Today Indians are citizens. Those American Indians who live on reservations set up by the federal government, however, do not have to pay state income taxes on earnings made on the reservation. But any income they make outside the reservation is subject to federal, state, and local taxes.

Section 2: The Census and House Representation

Section 2 also gives the government authority to take a United States census. The first census was taken in 1790, and a national census has been taken every ten years since then. This helps reshape congressional districts as the population changes.

The Constitution stated there should be no more than one representative for every 30,000 inhabitants. According to the 1920 census, there was one representative for every 243,013 people. If there had continued to be one representative for every 30,000 people, the House would today contain more than 8,000 members. In 1912, the size of House membership was set at 435 members. Each member of the House today represents approximately 572,000 people, although district sizes can vary widely even within one state.

Congress determines the number of representatives to which each state is entitled, but leaves it primarily up to the state legislatures to divide their respective states into congressional districts, each of which elects one representative.

States which have fewer than 572,000 inhabitants can have one representative.

Section 2: Speaker of the House

The Speaker is selected by a caucus, or special meeting, of the political party that has the majority (the most members). The House Speaker has the power to select who may speak from the floor, to refer bills (proposed laws) to committees, and to make numerous important decisions in the House. The Speaker may vote on issues but usually does not, except when there is a tie. Although presiding over debate, he or she may also enter into debates, after temporarily giving up the duties of acting as Speaker.

Section 2: Impeachment Power

The word impeachment is often misunderstood. It means the power to accuse and start formal charges of misconduct serious enough to result in possible removal from federal office. Impeachment by the House is similar to an indictment (formal accusation) by a grand jury in a criminal case. When a civil officer of the United States is accused of a crime, the House impeaches and the Senate holds the trial.

Impeachment is a two-step procedure. The House Judiciary Committee conducts a first investigation, then writes up a report explaining its findings. Then the entire House considers passing a resolution of impeachment. If this "carries," or is accepted, then the

Bill Clinton became the second president (and the first elected president) to be impeached in 1998.

House votes on detailed articles of impeachment. These are specific charges against the accused official.

Since the Constitution has been in place, the House has adopted impeachment resolutions against fourteen individuals. The most recent of these was President Bill Clinton, who was impeached by the House in 1998. The impeachment came about as a result of his actions during a scandal over his romantic relationship with a White House intern named Monica Lewinsky. Although the House impeached Clinton, the Senate did not convict him, and he remained in office to finish his term.

Section 3: The Senate

Each state has two senators. The Constitution originally provided for senators to be chosen by the legislatures of their states. The members of the state legislatures were expected to be able to make a more intelligent choice than the general public. As time went on, though, a growing discontent with this practice arose. Under the Seventeenth Amendment, adopted in 1913, United States senators are now elected by the ordinary voters of their states, just as members of the national House of Representatives are.

Section 3: Senate Elections

Senators serve six-year terms. One third of the senators stand for re-election (and possibly lose and leave office) every two years. The advantage is that at least two-thirds of the senators are always experienced members.

In order to make this possible, when the Constitution first went into effect, the Senate was divided into three groups: one third running for office for two years, one third running for office for four years, and one third running for office for six years.

Section 3: Qualifications of Senators

Senators are elected at large (by the whole state, rather than one district of it). There is nothing in the Constitution to prevent both senators of a certain state from living in the same city, on the same street, or even in the same house!

A senator must be at least thirty years old, have been a citizen of the United States for at least nine years, and must live in the state he or she will represent at the time of election. Senator's have higher age and longer citizenship qualifications compared to members of the House of Representatives. This indicates that the Framers of the Constitution wanted a mature and conservative body for the upper house of Congress.

Section 3: Vice President Presides over the Senate

The office of the vice president of the United States has a lot of prestige, but very little power. The only active duty of the vice president is service as the president of the Senate. The official title of the vice president when presiding over the Senate is "President of the Senate." He or she is, therefore, addressed in that body as "Mr. (or Ms.) President."

Even in this duty, however, the vice president's authority is not necessarily final. The Senate makes its own rules and may sometimes override the vice president. The vice president, in fact, has less power than any individual senator, because he or she can vote only in case of a tie. Of course, this vote in a tie situation may be extremely important.

Section 3: Other Senate Officers

The other officers of the Senate are similar to those of the House of Representatives. The president pro tempore (an officer elected to preside over the Senate when the vice president is not there) is always a senator. When the office of vice president becomes vacant, the president pro tempore receives the salary of the vice president of the United States. He or she also becomes permanent chair of the Senate if the vice president dies or becomes president of the United States.

The president pro tempore is chosen by the majority party. Usually, he or she is the member of the party who has served longest in the Senate. Unlike the vice president, the president pro tempore may, because he or she is a senator, vote on any issue.

Section 3: The Senate as a Court

In impeachment proceedings in the Senate against the president, the Chief Justice of the United States Supreme Court is required to preside. This is because the regular presiding officer of the Senate—the vice president of the United States—would have a direct interest in the outcome of the trial: should the president be found guilty and removed from office, the vice president would take over as president. The president pro tempore is also disqualified as the presiding officer because he or she is next in the line of succession to take over the presidency.

Two thirds of the Senate must agree in order to convict a person in an impeachment proceeding. Rarely does a case win such strong agreement that the accused is convicted. Even in the 1868 impeachment case of President Andrew Johnson, who was extremely unpopular with many senators because of his lenient treatment of the South after the Civil War, the Senate was still short one vote for conviction.

Section 3: Punishment in Cases of Impeachment

According to the Constitution, a person convicted on impeachment charges may be punished in one or both of two ways: He or she may be removed from office; or he or she may be removed from office and also be forever disqualified from again holding an office under the United States. After a person has been found guilty by the Senate on impeachment charges, he or she may be tried and punished by the courts. An officer of the United States may also be brought to trial in a court of law before being removed from office.

3

The Role of Congress, Article I, Sections 4–7

Organization of Congress

Section 4. The times, places and manner of holding elections for Senators and Representatives, shall be prescribed in each state by the legislature thereof; but the Congress may at any time by law make or alter such regulations, except as to the places of choosing Senators.

The Congress shall assemble at least once in every year, and such meeting shall be on the first Monday in December, unless they shall by law appoint a different day.

Section 5. Each House shall be the judge of the elections, returns and qualifications of its own members, and a majority of each shall constitute a quorum to do business; but a smaller number may adjourn from day to day, and may be authorized to compel the attendance of absent members, in such manner, and under such penalties as each House may provide.

Each House may determine the rules of its proceedings, punish its members for disorderly behavior, and, with the concurrence of two thirds, expel a member.

Each House shall keep a journal of its proceedings, and from time to time publish the same, excepting such parts as may in their judgment require secrecy; and the yeas and nays of the members of either House on any question shall, at the desire of one fifth of those present, be entered on the journal.

Neither House, during the session of Congress, shall, without the consent of the other, adjourn for more than three days, nor to any other place than that in which the two Houses shall be sitting.

Section 6. The Senators and Representatives shall receive a compensation for their services, to be ascertained by law, and paid out of the treasury of the United States. They shall in all cases, except treason, felony and breach of the peace, be privileged from arrest during their attendance at the session of their respective Houses, and in going to and returning from the same; and for any speech or debate in either House, they shall not be questioned in any other place.

No Senator or Representative shall, during the time for which he was elected, be appointed to any civil office under the authority of the United States, which shall have been created, or the emoluments whereof shall have been increased during such time: and no person holding any office under the United States, shall be a member of either House during his continuance in office.

Section 7. All bills for raising revenue shall originate in the House of Representatives; but the Senate may propose or concur with amendments as on other Bills.

Every bill which shall have passed the House of Representatives and the Senate, shall, before it become a law, be presented to the President of the United States; if he approve he shall sign it, but if not he shall return it, with his objections to that House in which it shall have originated, who shall enter the objections at large on their journal, and proceed to reconsider it. If after such reconsideration two thirds of that House shall agree to pass the bill, it shall be sent, together with the objections, to the other House, by which it shall likewise be reconsidered, and if approved by two thirds of that House, it shall become a law. But in all such cases the votes of both Houses shall be determined by yeas and nays, and the names of the persons voting for and against the bill shall be entered on the journal of each House respectively. If any bill shall not be returned by the President within ten days (Sundays excepted) after it shall have been presented to him, the same shall be a law, in like manner as if he had signed it, unless the Congress by their adjournment prevent its return, in which case it shall not be a law.

Every order, resolution, or vote to which the concurrence of the Senate and House of Representatives may be necessary (except on a question of adjournment) shall be presented to the President of the United States; and before the same shall take effect, shall be approved by him, or being disapproved by him, shall be repassed by two thirds of the Senate and House of Representatives, according to the rules and limitations prescribed in the case of a bill.

Rights and Duties of Congress

Sections 4 through 7 of Article 1 of the Constitution outline in great detail the specific rights and duties of Congress, while Section 8 explains the powers granted to Congress. These sections also explain the basic workings of the legislative department of the United States, outlining the Congress's rights and duties.

Section 4: Election and Meeting of Congress

Congress has, for the most part, left the time, place, and manner of holding elections to the state legislatures, which also determine who is qualified to vote for senators and representatives. Congress, however, has the power to change the states' decisions as to where, when, and how elections for federal offices are held.

Congress has made certain regulations. For example, Congress has set the time for the election of representatives to the House as the first Tuesday after the first Monday in November of even-numbered years. This is the rule except when another time is prescribed by state constitution.

Under an 1842 act of Congress, all states that are entitled to more than one seat in the House must elect their representatives by the district system. That is, each state is divided into congressional districts, and the voters of these districts vote for the individual candidates running to be representatives. This arrangement tries to give minority parties an opportunity to win some of the seats. If the entire state elected its representatives at large as is done for senators, the party with a majority in the state might easily win all the available seats.

Section 5: Organization and Rules of Each House

Each house of Congress has the power to judge the elections and qualifications of its own members. If the election of a member of either house is disputed, the house concerned has the final decision as to whether the "member" keeps his or her seat. This power, however, is limited. The house in question may not add qualifications for membership beyond those stated in the Constitution in order to reject or accept particular people.

There have been many cases in which candidates who claimed to be elected have been refused seats by Congress. The House and Senate have both denied duly elected persons their seats because they objected to them morally or politically. In 1900, for example, the House refused to seat Brigham H. Roberts, a Mormon from Utah, because he was a polygamist (had more than one wife at the same time).

Each house of Congress is given the power under the Constitution to make its own rules, punish its own members, and expel a member with a two-thirds vote. Once a member-elect has been seated, however, two thirds of a quorum (the number of members needed to do business) of the particular chamber must agree to expel a member. If only a majority vote were needed, members might be expelled for political reasons when the parties are closely divided and party feeling is running high.

Section 5: Rules of Proceedings

Each house makes its own rules and procedures. The House of Representatives generally adopts the rules of the previous House, making any changes later as it wishes. Because the Senate is a continuous body, it may change its rules whenever it sees fit.

Section 5: Keeping Record of Proceedings

An account of each day's proceedings in both houses of Congress is kept in the Journal. The Journal is usually published the next day. The Framers of the Constitution believed that the general public should be aware of the business and proceedings of Congress. The combined proceedings of the House and Senate are printed after each session in an official publication known as the *Congressional Record.*

Sometimes, Congress holds secret sessions. These secret sessions, not open to the public, are called "executive sessions." The most common reason for these is to discuss treaties in the Senate. The records of any executive sessions are kept separate from the general proceedings of Congress. They are not published in the *Congressional Record.*

By a curious custom, known as "leave to print," members of either house may extend their remarks without actually having to talk any longer. That is, a member may speak for just five minutes and then send to the Record a speech that would take an hour to read. As a result, much material appears in the Record that was never actually spoken on the floor of Congress.

At the end of every session, each House publishes a history of the bills and resolutions that came before it. Because of the sheer volume of material to be recorded for the use of the public, as well as the other works it publishes, the Government Printing Office is the largest printing establishment in the world.

Section 5: Methods of Voting

The houses of Congress have several ways for members to vote. *Viva voce,* or by voice is the most common method of voting. The Speaker of the House or the president of the Senate (the United States vice president) decides, by the volume of sound of the "yeas" (yes's) and "nays" (no's), which side has a greater number of votes.

A standing vote is also called "a division of the House." In this method, members stand or raise their hands to vote. If, in the opinion of a member of Congress, the judgment of the voice vote seems incorrect, he or she may call for a standing vote. As members stand or raise hands to express their votes, they are counted by the clerk for a precise measure of the vote.

A roll-call, or record vote, in the House takes a long time, but it prevents any possible fraud (effort to alter the vote unfairly) on the part of the Speaker. Each member's name is called alphabetically and the member votes aloud.

The roll-call method of voting in the House of Representatives was in force until 1973, when a new electronic voting system came into use. Now, a computer records the votes of members, replacing the traditional roll-call vote that required the clerk to count votes. The Senate has not deemed it necessary to use electronic voting devices because of its much smaller membership.

A very small number, one fifth of those present in the House, may demand a roll call on any question. Sometimes, the minority demands this method of voting merely to delay proceedings. The House of Representatives can avoid a roll-call vote by resolving itself into a Committee of the Whole. The Committee of the Whole is when the House decides to consider itself one large committee rather than the formal house of Congress it is. When the House sits as a Committee of the Whole, it may meet with one hundred members present (usually 218) to amend and act on bills. It also allows business to be handled less formally. The Speaker steps down and another member presides, but without the great power the Speaker normally holds.

When it comes to the question of overriding a presidential veto, the Constitution requires a roll-call vote.

Section 5: Adjournment

To become law, all bills must be passed by both houses. It would not be sensible, therefore, for one house to adjourn and leave the other in session. Neither would it be practical for one house to adjourn to Florida or California in the winter and to Maine in the summer while the other stayed in Washington, D.C. The Constitution, as a result, does not allow either house to adjourn for more than three days or to another place without the other house's consent.

Temporary adjournment for not more than three days may be taken for various reasons, for example, to consider bills in committee, to hold public hearings, or to show respect for a deceased colleague. Final adjournment at the end of the session is known as adjournment sine die, that is, adjournment without setting a day for resuming debate.

Section 6: Congressional Privileges and Restraints

Under the Articles of Confederation, the states paid their delegates to attend Congress. Salaries were not all the same. This practice tended to make the delegates give their first allegiance to their states. Now, under the Constitution's Article I, Section 6, all members of Congress are paid the same amount. The representatives and the senators are not dependent upon their state legislatures for their salaries. This is one of the privileges of congressional membership.

Many Americans objected to Congress's being paid by the federal treasury because it allows them to vote for and decide their own salaries. The payment of senators and representatives, however, was intended to show that members of Congress are national servants and not state officials, despite the fact that they represent state interests. To end public outcry over congressional pay raises, the Twenty-seventh Amendment was ratified. This amendment states that any pay increase voted by the members of Congress cannot go into effect until an election of representatives has passed. This allows the people to show their disapproval by voting out of office at least some of those who passed the pay raise.

Among their other privileges, senators and representatives are given freedom from arrest, with some exceptions. This privilege is designed so that no one can prevent members of Congress from attending the sessions of their respective houses. Without it, a member of Congress might be arrested and held on charges simply to prevent him or her from voting on a particular political issue. An exception to this rule is in cases of treason, felony, or a breach of peace. "Breach of peace" includes all criminal offenses.

Congress people also have the franking privilege— the right to send mail without postage. This privilege was given to members of Congress so that they would be able to send out information to anyone who wished to be informed or correspond with their congressional leaders. The president also enjoys this privilege.

A member of Congress needs to be able to say exactly what he or she thinks when debating important national issues. Therefore, although a member may be scolded by the Speaker of the House or Senate president for using ill-advised language, he or she cannot be sued in court for saying improper or offensive things. The floors of Congress are virtually the only places where a certain group of people (senators and representatives) is given the full benefits of the concept of "freedom of speech." "Ordinary" citizens of the United States do not have such broad freedom of speech. Anyone else may, in limited circumstances, be sued for saying inappropriate things. Congressional immunity, however, does not extend outside of Congress. In everyday life, members of Congress are subject to the same laws and limitations as other Americans.

Section 6: Holding Other Federal Offices

No senator or representative can be appointed to a civil position that was created while he or she was a member of Congress. In addition, he or she cannot take a position whose pay increased while the member was in Congress. Nor is a member of Congress allowed to hold a second United States Office. The Constitution also forbids any person holding a federal office from being a member of Congress. This prevents a member of Congress from being the head of an administrative department.

Section 7: How a Bill Becomes a Law

Most of the actual work of preparing bills is done in committees. Each house has a number of regular or standing (permanent) committees.

Any member of the House of Representatives may introduce a bill by placing it in a basket (the "hopper") on the clerk's desk. The clerk then refers each bill to the appropriate standing committee. Important bills are usually introduced by the committee chair.

In the Senate, on the other hand, any member may rise and announce an intention of introducing a bill. The proposed legislation is then sent to the appropriate committee by the Senate's clerk. A bill passed by one house is then sent to the other house, where it goes through the same procedures. If the bill is amended in any way by the second house, it must be returned to the house from which it originated. If the house where the bill started does not agree to the changes, a conference committee is appointed, with each house being equally represented. The conference committee adjusts the disputed points, and the revised bill is then presented to each house for a final vote.

A "bill" is the technical name of a measure introduced in either house of Congress until it has been passed by that house. At that point, it is reprinted as an "act", that is, an act of one house of Congress. The term *act*, however, is also popularly used to refer to a measure that has been passed by both houses and has become law.

Section 7: Passage or Veto

One of four things may happen to any bill that has been passed by both the House and the Senate: First, the president may sign it and it becomes a law. Second, the president may refuse to sign it, in which case he is said to have vetoed it. In this case the bill may still be passed over the veto if two thirds of the membership of each house agree to accept it without any changes.

The third possibility occurs if the president does not return the bill within ten days (Sundays and holidays excepted) to the house from which it originated. In this case, the bill becomes law even without the president's signature. The president sometimes allows a bill to become a law in this way, when he or she objects to a certain part of the bill but does not want to hold up the bill as a whole.

The fourth possible outcome for a bill is the so-called "pocket veto." If a bill is sent to the president within ten days of Congress's adjournment, he or she does not have to take the trouble to veto it to avoid approving it. The president can merely lay it aside (put it in a pocket, so to speak). The bill is automatically "dead" if Congress adjourns within ten working days of the day the president receives the bill. This may not apply if the house where the bill originated authorizes an officer to receive presidential vetoes during the time the chamber is not in session. Nor does the pocket veto apply to recesses during a congressional session or even to adjournments between congressional sessions.

The line-item veto became law on January 1, 1997. This law gives the president the power to reject parts of bills without rejecting bills in their entirety. The line-item veto faces challenges in court to determine its constitutionality.

After a bill has been approved by both houses of Congress and signed by the president, it is delivered to the State Department. There, it gets a serial number. The original copies of all laws are preserved in the Division of Research and Publications in the State Department. Laws are published in annual volumes of the *Statutes-at-Large*.

Section 7: Congress and the Veto Power

The Constitution prevents Congress from passing a bill without the president's signature by calling it an order, resolution, or a vote, rather than a bill. A joint resolution of Congress (for example, a declaration of war), however, has the force of law and must be given to the president for approval.

When two thirds of the membership of each house of Congress agrees to a proposal for an amendment to the Constitution, it is submitted to the states for ratification (acceptance) immediately. It is not sent to the president for approval first. In cases dealing with constitutional amendments, Congress functions under powers granted in the Constitution's Article V. In order to become effective, the proposed amendment needs the concurrence (agreement) of three fourths of the states, but not of the president.

In the 1930s, under the administration of President Franklin D. Roosevelt, and in the 1970s, Congress made use of the "concurrent resolution." These resolutions are statements made by the separate houses of Congress at the same time to show that they hold the same opinion. They may also want to show Congress's authority to the president. When powers are granted to the president in an original bill, Congress may state that those powers will last until they are taken away by a concurrent resolution. By so doing, Congress may take away powers it had previously granted without passing a new law that would be subject to presidential veto.

The Powers of Congress, Article I, Section 8

The Powers of Congress

Section 8. The Congress shall have power to lay and collect taxes, duties, imposts and excises, to pay the debts and provide for the common defense and general welfare of the United States; but all duties, imposts and excises shall be uniform throughout the United States;

To borrow money on the credit of the United States;

To regulate commerce with foreign nations, and among the several states, and with the Indian tribes;

To establish a uniform rule of naturalization, and uniform laws on the subject of bankruptcies throughout the United States;

To coin money, regulate the value thereof, and of foreign coin, and fix the standard of weights and measures;

To provide for the punishment of counterfeiting the securities and current coin of the United States;

To establish post offices and post roads;

To promote the progress of science and useful arts, by securing for limited times to authors and inventors the exclusive right to their respective writings and discoveries;

To constitute tribunals inferior to the Supreme Court;

To define and punish piracies and felonies committed on the high seas, and offenses against the law of nations;

To declare war, grant letters of marque and reprisal, and make rules concerning captures on land and water;

To raise and support armies, but no appropriation of money to that use shall be for a longer term than two years;

To provide and maintain a navy;

To make rules for the government and regulation of the land and naval forces;

To provide for calling forth the militia to execute the laws of the union, suppress insurrections and repel invasions;

To provide for organizing, arming, and disciplining, the militia, and for governing such part of them as may be employed in the service of the United States, reserving to the states respectively, the appointment of the officers, and the authority of training the militia according to the discipline prescribed by Congress;

To exercise exclusive legislation in all cases whatsoever, over such District (not exceeding ten miles square) as may, by cession of particular states, and the acceptance of Congress, become the seat of the government of the United States, and to exercise like authority over all places purchased by the consent of the legislature of the state in which the same shall be, for the erection of forts, magazines, arsenals, dockyards, and other needful buildings;—And

To make all laws which shall be necessary and proper for carrying into execution the foregoing powers, and all other powers vested by this Constitution in the government of the United States, or in any department or officer thereof.

The Powers of Congress

Article I of the Constitution covers a broad area. It not only discusses qualifications for becoming a member of Congress and how the houses of Congress should function, but also specifies the many powers granted to Congress under the Constitution.

The Taxing Power

Section 8 states that Congress has the power to lay taxes. Tax is a general term. Any sum of money paid to support the government is a tax. The word taxes includes duties, imposts, and excises. A "duty" is a monetary obligation to a government. An "impost" is a tax on imports or exports. An "excise" tax is placed on so-called "luxury items," that are not necessary for survival, but rather are "extras," such as tobacco, liquor, jewelry, and fur coats. Several other items, which some would argue are "necessary," such as automobiles and gasoline, are also subject to excise taxes. Excise taxes are also imposed on the performance of certain acts, engaging in some occupations, or enjoying some privileges. Excise taxes are also called "internal revenue taxes." They are specifically placed to collect money with which to run the government.

A protective tariff is a tax placed on goods made in foreign countries in order to raise the price of those items. For example, imported Swiss cheese has a protective tax put on it when it enters the United States.

The tax is added to the cost of the cheese and thereby raises the price. Lawmakers hope the citizens of the United States will buy less expensive domestic items, promoting home industry. This does not always happen, however. Some foreign countries are able to make items, transport them, pay a tax, and still sell their goods cheaper than the same product made at home. A tariff is not considered a revenue because its purpose is to "protect" home industries by underselling foreign-made products, not to raise money for the government.

Direct taxes include poll taxes, real estate taxes, and income taxes. Indirect taxes, on the other hand, are usually included as part of the price paid for goods or services. Examples of these are the excise taxes paid on liquor, tobacco, drugs, and gasoline and import duties on foreign goods.

Providing for the General Welfare

The Constitution states that Congress has the power to tax so it may raise enough money to provide for the general welfare of the American people. Through the years, and with ever-changing times, the concept of the "general welfare" has been stretched and increased. Congress taxes and spends hundreds of millions of dollars every year to provide funds for education, agriculture, and business; to aid in the care of the poor, the aged, and the disabled; and to help reduce unemployment. The federal government has numerous "grants-in-aid" programs. These account for about 25 percent of the funds spent by states and local governments. In order to receive such grants, Congress normally sets conditions. Congress may require the states to match some of the federal funds to create agencies to administer the programs. Another condition may be to submit plans to federal officials, or to allow federal inspection so Congress can be sure aid programs meet federal standards.

Uniform Duties

The Constitution requires that all federal duties, imposts, and excises be the same throughout the United States. That is, if a tax of two cents a pound is laid on imported coffee, two cents must be collected on this article in every port. It would be illegal to collect one cent in Baltimore, MD, and three cents in New Orleans, LA.

The Borrowing Power

Congress has the power to borrow money on the credit of the United States. The federal government borrows money by selling interest-bearing bonds and short-term (treasury) certificates. These are free from state and municipal taxation.

There are no limits placed on Congress as to how much money it may borrow or spend. Congress alone sets its limits to make the national budget. Therefore, Congress also controls the national debt (how much the United States owes).

Regulating Commerce

The Constitution allows Congress to regulate both foreign and interstate commerce (trade). Its power in this respect is practically unlimited. Congress has even gone so far as to stop foreign trade. When Great Britain and France were at war during the early years of the nineteenth century, they often attacked the ships of the United States, even though Americans had declared themselves neutral in the conflict. To try to protect American shipping, as well as to punish Great Britain and France, Congress, during the administration of

President Thomas Jefferson signed the Embargo Act into
law, halting commerce with foreign nations.

President Thomas Jefferson, passed the Embargo Act of 1807. This law made it illegal for the United States to trade with foreign nations. Although the law was repealed soon after, it showed just how broad the powers of Congress over trade can be.

The power to regulate foreign and interstate commerce has enormously expanded the authority of the federal government. A few examples of the broad use Congress has made of this clause include protective tariffs, railroad regulation, anti-trust legislation, pure food and drug acts, and the restriction of immigration.

The word *commerce* has extremely varied meanings. Over the years, it has been extended to cover all forms of transportation and communication. Under its power to regulate commerce, Congress works to prevent misleading advertising, establishes frequencies for radio stations, protects migrating birds, and makes kidnapping a federal offense.

Chief Justice John Marshall made it clear in the Supreme Court's 1824 *Gibbons* v. *Ogden* ruling that Congress's power over commerce carries with it the power to enforce its regulations. Marshall stated that the commerce power "is complete in itself, may be exercised to its utmost extent, and acknowledges no limitations, other than are prescribed in the constitution."[1]

Congress has used its powers over commerce to affect the African slave trade, lottery tickets, alcoholic beverages, stolen automobiles, and impure foods. It has also imposed its commerce powers to stop the transportation of products made or transported by companies that do not pay their employees at least the minimum wage. Congress used this same power to pass the Civil Rights Act of 1964. This monumental law forbids discrimination because of race, religion, or national origin in public places. It also forbids

Thomas Gibbons was the plaintiff in the landmark case of Gibbons v. Ogden.

discrimination because of sex in employment.[2]

In 1969, the Supreme Court upheld the use of the Civil Rights Act in the case of *Daniel* v. *Paul,* which involved a recreational "club" that used materials produced outside its state and was open to travelers from other states. Using its commerce power, the Supreme Court said that the club could not discriminate against customers on account of race.[3] By using the commerce clause in this way Congress is able to affect intrastate (within one state) activities in the smallest town that practices racial discrimination, if it uses goods from out of state.

Congress also has full power over "navigable waters of the United States." This includes those waters that may be made navigable by "reasonable improvements."

The Supreme Court has stated that such waters "are subject to national planning and control: Flood protection, watershed development, recovery of the cost of improvements through utilization of power are . . . parts of commerce control."[4]

Rules of Naturalization

Section 8, Clause 4 of Article I gives Congress the power to make laws determining how foreign immigrants may become citizens. By the same token, Congress has the right to determine which foreign people may enter the United States, and for what purposes.

Congress also has the power to regulate immigration, and has been given considerable authority to regulate the conduct of aliens (non-citizens) living within the United States. Because aliens live in the United States by the will of the government, they may also be removed by the government. However, while they are living in the United States, Congress may not deprive aliens of many of the rights granted to American citizens, such as freedom of worship, speech, and fair trials, although aliens do not have the right to vote or hold federal office. Federal policy states that aliens may not be deported (sent out of the United States) if they entered the country legally and became public charges because of causes that arose after they entered. While in the United States, "they are entitled to the full and equal benefit of all state laws for the security of persons and property."[5]

Coinage, Weights, and Measures

Congress's power to coin and regulate money is interpreted to mean issuing paper money as well as gold and silver certificates, United States notes, treasury notes, and Federal Reserve notes, in addition to actual metal coins.

Congress also determines what rates of exchange should be for foreign money when it is accepted by the United States Treasury in payment for debt. Congress, however, has never interfered in rates of exchange in private contracts between American citizens and citizens of a foreign country. Payment in these cases is regulated by the current market rate of foreign currency exchanges.

Punishing Counterfeiters

Counterfeiting is the crime of making fake coins or forging paper money, bonds, or other government securities. Congress has the power to provide for counterfeiters to be punished. The Treasury Department maintains a force of secret service agents to prevent counterfeiting.

Postal Service

Congress has the power to "establish Post Offices." These words have been interpreted to give Congress every conceivable authority over the mail. Congress not only establishes post offices, but also builds post offices, although the United States Postal Service today is actually an independent government agency. Interfering with the mail is considered a serious federal offense.

Copyrights and Patents

Congress has the power to issue copyrights and patents to protect the rights of authors and other artists and inventors. Copyright provisions cover pictures and musical compositions, as well as literary productions. A copyright gives a writer or artist the exclusive right to make, distribute, and otherwise control copies of his or her work. Congress provides for the protection of works by authors, musicians, and artists by copyright. To inventors it provides protection by patent. A patent is the exclusive right to make, sell, or use an invention.

The first federal copyright law was enacted in 1790. It protected original maps, charts, and books. Revisions of the law were made in 1831, 1870, and 1909. These last revisions were based on the fact that the printing press was the primary means of spreading information. However, over the course of the twentieth century, many technological advances in communication media, such as radio, television, and film, came into wide use. Therefore, a major revision was made on January 1, 1978.

A copyright issued before 1978 is granted for twenty-eight years. During the last year, it may be renewed for forty-seven more years. Copyrights granted after January 1, 1978, are valid until fifty years after the creator of the work has died. A copyright passes to the creator's heirs after his or her death.

A patent, on the other hand, is valid for twenty years. A patent may be renewed by an act of Congress, but to date, no patent has ever been renewed. Like copyrights, patents are part of a person's estate and go to his or her heirs at the time of death. Anonymous works and those made by an employee for an employer, are protected for seventy-five years from the date of the first publication or one hundred years from the year of creation, whichever expires first.

If someone believes that a work has been infringed upon, he or she must have had the work registered with the Register of Copyrights in order to sue. If a work is published without a copyright notice, then the author must register the work within five years of the publication. Otherwise, copyright protection is lost.

Punishing Piracy

Piracy is robbery on the high seas. Under the Constitution, Congress has the power to punish pirates. Pirates are considered enemies of all nations. As such they may be captured and brought into the jurisdiction of United States federal courts. Piracies and felonies on the high seas and violations of international law are not crimes against individual states. Piracy is an offense against the law of all nations. The trial of these crimes is handled by the federal government.

Declaring War

Declaring war, like the taxing power, is too important and dangerous to be given to any one person. Therefore, the people, through their representatives in Congress, have the power to declare war.

War may be declared by a simple joint resolution (a declaration of war) of both houses of Congress seated jointly. The resolution must be approved by the president.

The concept behind this clause of the Constitution has its origins in England. There, the king had the power to declare war without consulting the legislature or the people. The Framers of the United States Constitution wanted to transfer that power from the president to Congress.

Despite this provision, wars in which the United States has been engaged have always been entered with executive action. That is, the president normally goes before a joint session of Congress and requests that war be declared.

Letters of Marque and Reprisal

Congress has the power to grant letters of marque and reprisal. These were licenses issued to private citizens (mainly shipowners) during wartime, allowing them to arm their ships with guns to help the navy attack the enemy.

There were many privateers (these privately owned armed ships) during the American Revolution and the War of 1812. Now, however, war has changed so much that it is doubtful whether Congress will ever authorize privateers in the future.

Interestingly, during World War II, Congress granted author Ernest Hemingway permission to use his private vessel, the Pilar, as a privateer to seek out and attack German U-boats, or submarines. Hemingway actually had his ship armed with an assortment of weapons including fifty-caliber machine guns, bazookas, grenades, and short-fused bombs. It was reported that he spotted one U-boat far out on the horizon but he was unable to catch up with it before it disappeared. This is said to have been his only reported "encounter" with an enemy vessel.

The Army

Congress has the power to raise an army. To raise an army quickly (especially in times of war) the federal government has in the past used the draft (also called conscription). In 1940, before the United States entered World War II, Congress passed the first peacetime draft law in American history. Under this measure, men between the ages of eighteen and forty-five became liable for military service.

In addition to the power to draft soldiers, Congress has the power to commandeer (take over) materials for the armed forces, set price ceilings (limits on how high prices may be raised), allocate (assign) and ration materials; and direct the production, marketing, and consumption of all products. In short, Congress has the power to do whatever it believes "necessary and proper" for carrying out a war successfully.

The Navy

Congress has made many rules for governing and regulating the land and naval forces as different circumstances have arisen. The great length of the American coastline, the extent of foreign trade, and the distant locations of United States island possessions, are some of the main reasons for keeping a large navy as the nation's first line of defense. Unlike the army, the Framers did not see the navy as a threat to the people's liberty. For that reason, no limitations were put on naval appropriations. This is practical, too, because the building of naval vessels often takes much longer than two years. The freedom to make appropriations over time allows funds for ship construction to be pledged well in advance.

Regulating the Armed Forces

Under the Constitution, the president is the Commander in Chief of the army and navy. Congress, however, has the power to make all laws regulating the military and naval establishments, and to provide the funds for their upkeep.

In 1947, a bill was passed that united the armed forces under the overall supervision of a Cabinet officer called the secretary of defense. The involvement of an executive officer allows the president to share the power of Congress in regard to the military. However, the armed forces are still subject to specific constitutional limitations. Military personnel, for example, do not have exactly the same constitutional freedoms as civilians do. They live under their own strict code of laws enacted by Congress known as the General Articles of the Uniform Code of Military Justice.

Calling Out and Regulating Militia

All able-bodied men between the ages of eighteen and forty-five are automatically included in the unorganized militia of each state. Congress has laid down general rules for organizing, arming, and disciplining the militia. The states, however, are the ones that carry out these rules. The organized voluntary militia, known as the National Guard, is made up of those citizens who have enrolled to undergo military training at specific intervals. The separate state units of the National Guard are considered a part of the nation's military establishment. The president becomes the Commander in Chief of any militia called into the actual service of the United States. The organization, equipment, and training of the National Guard are supervised by the War department, and its expenses are paid by the federal government.

The militia may be called for three purposes: to carry out the laws of the Union, to suppress insurrections (rebellions against the government), and to repel invasions by foreign powers. In 1794, President George Washington called out the militias of Pennsylvania, Virginia, and other states to suppress the Whiskey Rebellion, an uprising of farmers who were protesting a tax on whiskey. The militia was also called out to help the United States fight Great Britain in the War of 1812. President Abraham Lincoln called out the militia of all the states at the beginning of the Civil War in 1861. Other than these incidents, however, there has rarely been a need to use the militia nationally.

Because of its nature as a domestic force, the militia may not be sent out of the country. Therefore, it was not used in the Mexican War of 1846–1848, the Spanish-American War of 1898, or either of the two World Wars.

At times, the governors of states have called on their state militia, or National Guard, when they felt it was necessary to maintain order or enforce laws. The National Guard was used several times in state crises during the civil rights movement of the 1950s and

President Abraham Lincoln showed strong use of his executive power during the Civil War.

1960s. Sometimes, it was called to help prevent violence when schools and other facilities were integrated. Some governors, however, called out the National Guard to try to keep public schools segregated by race. For example, Governor Orval Faubus of Arkansas used the National Guard to keep African-American students from trying to attend Little Rock's Central High School in 1957.

The militia has been called out in times of urban riots to prevent injury and looting. It may also be used in times of disaster, such as earthquakes and floods, to help keep order.

The president may, in case of "necessity," declare "martial law." This means military personnel are put in charge of enforcing civil law. "Necessity" may include such situations as riots or natural disasters that cause severe destruction.

Areas Under Control of Congress

In 1789, New York City was the capital of the United States. Philadelphia served as headquarters from 1790 until 1800, when the newly built city of Washington, in the District of Columbia, became the permanent capital. The District, which now has an area of about seventy square miles, was given to the nation in 1790 by Maryland and Virginia.

Under the Constitution, Congress directly represents the District of Columbia. Originally, the president, with the approval of the Senate, appointed the board of three commissioners who serve as the District's administrative authority. Congress has created a system of courts for the District. Residents of the District of Columbia have the right to vote in national elections and have three electoral votes in presidential elections.

The idea of having the national capital located in an area that is not part of any state was intended to keep the capital free from the interference of state or municipal officials.

The "Elastic Clause"

The last clause of Article IV, Section 8, dealing with the implied powers of Congress, is known as the elastic clause. Also called the "necessary and proper clause," it deals with implied powers that give Congress the right to make any laws it considers "necessary and proper" for carrying out its specifically stated powers.

This clause allows Congress to "stretch" the meaning of the Constitution to make the laws it wants. The elastic clause and the doctrine of implied powers have made possible a great expansion of the activities of the federal government in response to changing needs over time.

In 1787, as the Framers knew, it would have been impossible for any group to foresee every detail that might arise for the government. If the Framers had tried to do such a thing, thousands of congressional powers would have been described in Section 8. Instead, there are only seventeen short paragraphs defining the powers of Congress.

If Congress had been limited by the powers expressly mentioned in Section 8, it could not have enacted many of the programs it has passed through American history. To allow Congress to perform its duties well, the Supreme Court ruled from the first years of the Constitution that Congress has not only those powers expressly granted, but also powers that may be implied from the expressed powers.

Some people interpret the phrase "necessary and

proper" strictly. These people emphasize the word *necessary*. They are known as "strict constructionists" because they wish to limit the federal government to the powers specified in the Constitution itself.

Those who interpret the phrase loosely, on the other hand, to extend the power of federal government, emphasize the word *proper*. They are called "loose constructionists." Alexander Hamilton, the first secretary of the treasury, was one such loose constructionist. He argued for the creation of the Bank of the United States, even though the power to make a bank was not written in the Constitution. Hamilton said it was implied as necessary and proper. Since Congress had the right to levy and collect taxes, there had to be a place to hold these federal monies. Greatly through the influence of loose constructionists, Congress has been allowed to increase its power significantly over the years the Constitution has been in effect.

5

Denied Powers, Article I, Section 9–10

Powers Forbidden to Congress

Section 9. The migration or importation of such persons as any of the states now existing shall think proper to admit, shall not be prohibited by the Congress prior to the year one thousand eight hundred and eight, but a tax or duty may be imposed on such importation, not exceeding ten dollars for each person.

The privilege of the writ of *habeas corpus* shall not be suspended, unless when in cases of rebellion or invasion the public safety may require it.

No bill of attainder or ex post facto Law shall be passed.

No capitation, or other direct, tax shall be laid, unless in proportion to the census or enumeration herein before directed to be taken.

No tax or duty shall be laid on articles exported from any state.

No preference shall be given by any regulation of commerce or revenue to the ports of one state over those of another: nor shall vessels bound to, or from, one state, be obliged to enter, clear or pay duties in another.

No money shall be drawn from the treasury, but in consequence of appropriations made by law; and a regular statement and account of receipts and expenditures of all public money shall be published from time to time.

No title of nobility shall be granted by the United States: and no person holding any office of profit or trust under them, shall, without the consent of the Congress, accept of any present, emolument, office, or title, of any kind whatever, from any king, prince, or foreign state.

Powers Forbidden to the States

Section 10. No state shall enter into any treaty, alliance, or confederation; grant letters of marque and reprisal; coin money; emit bills of credit; make anything but gold and silver coin a tender in payment of debts; pass any bill of attainder, ex post facto law, or law impairing the obligation of contracts, or grant any title of nobility.

No state shall, without the consent of the Congress, lay any imposts or duties on imports or exports, except what may be absolutely necessary for executing its inspection laws: and the net produce of all duties and imposts, laid by any state on imports or exports, shall be for the use of the treasury of the United States; and all such laws shall be subject to the revision and control of the Congress.

No state shall, without the consent of Congress, lay any duty of tonnage, keep troops, or ships of war in time of peace, enter into any agreement or compact with another state, or with a foreign power, or engage in war, unless actually invaded, or in such imminent danger as will not admit of delay.

Section 9: Denied Powers

Article I, Section 8, lists the things Congress can do, Section 9 states the things Congress is *forbidden* to do.

At the Constitutional Convention held in Philadelphia in 1787, the representatives of the Southern slaveholding states refused to give Congress full control over foreign commerce. They feared anti-slavery Northerners might demand an immediate stop to the importation of African slaves. The delegates, therefore, agreed to a compromise.

Section 9: The Slave Trade

The Framers agreed that Congress would not be allowed to forbid the importation of new African slaves into the thirteen original states before the year 1808, although the word slave was never actually mentioned. The Constitution referred to imported slaves as "Persons . . . any of the States now existing shall think proper to admit." In 1807, Congress passed a law ending new international slave traffic. The entire clause, however, was later voided in 1865 by the Thirteenth Amendment, which prohibited slavery in the United States and all its possessions.

Section 9: Habeas Corpus

A writ of *habeas corpus* is a legal document that forces a warden to release a person held in prison unless he or she has been formally charged with a crime or has been convicted in a court of law. The writ is a court order directing a sheriff, warden, or other law officer to bring the person held as prisoner to court so that a judge may decide whether continued detention is lawful. The purpose of this is to protect citizens from arrests and detention without lawful reason, such as those based on dislike or suspicion.

Habeas Corpus does not free an accused person permanently. It just brings such a person to court. President Abraham Lincoln suspended the writ in 1861 because of the crisis of the Civil War and the fear of Southern spies sabotaging the North's war efforts. Mainly, he suspended *habeas corpus* to combat the

A strong fear of communism, which was perceived as a menacing threat to the freedom of the American government, led some politicians to act without proper regard for the Constitution.

activities of "Copperheads" (Northerners who were sympathetic to the South and worked to end the war). Despite the apparent urgency of the crisis, Lincoln was bitterly attacked for suspending this basic right of the people.

Section 9: Bills of Attainder

A bill of attainder is a legislative act that punishes a person or group of people without first holding a trial. This is prohibited by the Constitution. Although Congress has the power to define a crime, it may not carry out punishment. That is the right of a court of law.

In the early years of the United States, the definition of what could be considered a bill of attainder was expanded to include imprisonment, banishment, confiscation of property, denial of jobs, and other kinds of punishments. These are no longer legal.

Two challenges to the bill of attainder were the case of *United States* v. *Lovett*[1] and the 1965 case of *United States* v. *Brown*.[2] The second case challenged a provision stating that any member of the Communist party would not be allowed to serve as a trade union officer. The Supreme Court ruled in both of these cases that Congress had passed illegal bills of attainder because they inflicted punishment, that is, the loss of a job on specific persons or on members of a certain political group.

Section 9: Ex Post Facto Laws

An *ex post facto* law is one that applies to an act committed before the law was passed. The law makes the punishment for a crime more severe than it was when the crime was committed, or changes the proof needed to convict. On the other hand, it does not prevent the passage of penal laws that would benefit the accused, by decreasing or making punishment less severe.[3]

Section 9: Taxes in Proportion to Population

A capitation tax is a poll, or head, tax. It is a tax that a person is required to pay when he or she votes. Such taxes have never been levied by the United States federal government. The states, on the other hand, have sometimes levied poll taxes as a voting requirement. This was often done in the years after the Civil War as a method to prevent African Americans or poor people, who often could not afford to pay the tax, from voting.

In 1894, Congress levied a second income tax. The legality of this tax was appealed to the Supreme Court, and in 1895, the tax was declared unconstitutional. To be legal, the court declared, it would have to be apportioned among the states according to population. To eliminate the issue and allow the federal government to levy an income tax, the Sixteenth Amendment, which expressly allows a federal income tax, was ratified in 1913.

Section 9: Export Taxes

The taxing and spending powers of the federal government are limited. The Framers made sure of this in order to prevent taxation falling more heavily on one part of the country than on another, and to discourage (but not necessarily prevent) the misuse of public funds.

Congress is forbidden to tax goods exported from the states. However, it can regulate commerce.

Before the Constitution, while the United States was governed by the Articles of Confederation,

After the Civil War, many African Americans were able to vote for the first time in their lives. Unfortunately, the violent attitudes of racist whites would not allow them to enjoy their new civil rights for long.

commercial relations were so bad between the states that the Framers of the Constitution determined it was important to put an end to interstate commercial rivalries and tariffs on goods passing between the states. Before the Constitution strengthened the national government, Americans were loyal to their home states, but not necessarily to the nation as a whole. In fact, different states were almost like foreign countries. States felt no need to cooperate with one another, especially in regard to trade.

The Constitution, therefore, gave Congress the power to regulate interstate commerce as well as trade with foreign nations. This prevented the states from discriminating against each other. By the same token, Congress may not discriminate against the trade of a certain state or group of states.

Section 9: Money without Appropriations or Secrecy in Finances

Neither the president nor any other government official can go into the treasury and take funds for any purpose. Government money may not be spent unless it is approved by a law passed by Congress. The legislative branch thus has full control of the "purse strings." In this way, Congress gains some control over all branches of the federal government, since all departments need the money Congress can provide if they hope to function.

In 1921, Congress created the General Accounting Office, headed by the Comptroller General. This person is essentially the bookkeeper, or accountant, of the United States government. This official, who reports directly to Congress, checks all expenditures.

Section 9: Titles of Nobility

When the Constitution was written, there was strong feeling against noble titles. Titles went against the ideas expressed in the Declaration of Independence, which said that "all men are created equal." Therefore, the Framers of the Constitution made it illegal for the government of the United States to grant titles to American citizens.

Congress, however, has the right to remove this restriction at any time. In fact, it has done so. For example, members of the American Expeditionary

Forces (military units that fought in the World War I) were allowed to receive decorations presented by the other Allied powers of World Wars I and II and other conflicts, even though those decorations gave the recipients, American citizens, noble titles.

As a check against bribery of officials by foreign powers, the Constitution also states that no federal official may accept any title or other award from a foreign state without the consent of Congress. Such consent usually is given in the form of a joint resolution, which designates by name those officers and government employees who may accept decorations, orders, medals, or presents already awarded them by foreign governments.

Section 10: Powers Denied to the States

In Article IV, Section 9, the Constitution tells what Congress and the federal government are forbidden to do. Similarly, Section 10 tells what the states may not do. The powers mentioned in this paragraph are those that may be exercised by the federal government alone.

Section 10: Contracts

The states are forbidden to pass bills of attainder, ex post facto laws, or to grant titles of nobility. Although the treaty-making power naturally belongs to the federal government, states may make compromises with one another, as long as they deal with subjects that concern the states alone, and do not affect the power of the federal government. The Constitution says, "No state shall pass any law impairing [changing or harming] the Obligation of Contracts."

Many volumes have been written about contracts and contract law, but the general meaning of the clause is: States may pass laws regulating future contracts, but they may not pass ex post facto laws (already completed and agreed to). The word contracts referred to those made between individuals, especially contracts of debt. Obligations arising from these contracts could not be changed by state law. Over the years, the clause has come to include contracts made by states themselves, including franchises granted to corporations.

Section 10: May Not Wage War

All matters concerning troops and ships of war are placed in the hands of Congress, not the states, just as the treaty-making power is left to the president and the Senate. A state may not engage in war unless it is actually invaded. In such a case, it may use all its resources to defend itself. The military restrictions on the several states were designed chiefly for the following purposes: to emphasize national control over foreign relations and defense measures; to prevent civil conflicts between states or between a state and the federal government; and to avoid state policies that might involve the entire nation in war with a foreign country.

6

The Executive Branch, Article II, Section 1

The Executive Branch

Section 1. The executive power shall be vested in a President of the United States of America. He shall hold his office during the term of four years, and, together with the Vice President, chosen for the same term, be elected, as follows:

Each state shall appoint, in such manner as the Legislature thereof may direct, a number of electors, equal to the whole number of Senators and Representatives to which the State may be entitled in the Congress: but no Senator or Representative, or person holding an office of trust or profit under the United States, shall be appointed an elector.

The electors shall meet in their respective states, and vote by ballot for two persons, of whom one at least shall not be an inhabitant of the same state with themselves. And they shall make a list of all the persons voted for, and of the number of votes for each; which list they shall sign and certify, and transmit sealed to the seat of the government of the United States, directed to the President of the Senate. The President of the Senate shall, in the presence of the Senate and House of Representatives, open all the certificates, and the votes shall then be counted. The person having the greatest number of votes shall be the President, if such number be a majority of the whole number of electors appointed; and if there be more than one who have such majority, and have an equal number of votes, then the House of Representatives shall immediately choose by ballot one of them for President; and if no person have a majority, then from the five highest on the list the said House shall in like manner choose the President. But in choosing the President, the votes shall be taken by States, the representation from each state having one vote; A quorum for this purpose shall consist of a member or members from two thirds of the states, and a majority of all the states shall be necessary to a choice. In every case, after the choice of the President, the person having the greatest number of votes of the electors shall be the Vice President. But if there should remain two or more who have equal votes, the Senate shall choose from them by ballot the Vice President.

The Congress may determine the time of choosing the electors, and the day on which they shall give their votes; which day shall be the same throughout the United States.

No person except a natural born citizen, or a citizen of the United States, at the time of the adoption of this Constitution, shall be eligible to the office of President; neither shall any person be eligible to that office who shall not have attained to the age of thirty five years, and been fourteen Years a resident within the United States.

In case of the removal of the President from office, or of

his death, resignation, or inability to discharge the powers and duties of the said office, the same shall devolve on the Vice President, and the Congress may by law provide for the case of removal, death, resignation or inability, both of the President and Vice President, declaring what officer shall then act as President, and such officer shall act accordingly, until the disability be removed, or a President shall be elected.

The President shall, at stated times, receive for his services, a compensation, which shall neither be increased nor diminished during the period for which he shall have been elected, and he shall not receive within that period any other emolument from the United States, or any of them.

Before he enter on the execution of his office, he shall take the following oath or affirmation: "I do solemnly swear (or affirm) that I will faithfully execute the office of President of the United States, and will to the best of my ability, preserve, protect and defend the Constitution of the United States."

Article II: The Executive Branch

Article II of the Constitution deals with the Executive Branch. Under the Articles of Confederation, both executive and legislative power was left to Congress. But it soon became clear that the executive power should not be left in the hands of a large body of representatives who had to debate and vote on every issue. So, when the Constitution was written, the Framers established the presidency. It was modeled not after the kings of Europe but after the governorships of the states. The Framers were certain that George Washington, who was the best known and respected

Popular Revolutionary leader George Washington was elected to be the first president of the United States.

leader in the United States, would be the country's first president. This fact reassured the people that no tyranny would be established during his, the first, presidential administration.

Section 1: Term of the President

At first, the members of the Constitutional Convention proposed to make the president's term seven years, and not to allow the president to run for re-election. By the final draft of the Constitution, however, the length of the term had been reduced to four years, and the Constitution remained silent as to whether (and how many times) a president might be reelected.

Until 1940, when President Franklin D. Roosevelt ran for and won a third term, tradition, first established by George Washington, limited a president to two terms. Franklin D. Roosevelt actually won a fourth term, but he died in office near the beginning of this term in April 1945. In 1951, the Twenty-second Amendment to the Constitution limited all future presidents to two terms.

Section 1: Presidential Electors

The Philadelphia Convention had trouble deciding how the president should be chosen. A proposal to have the president selected directly by Congress was voted down. The fear of this proposal was that if Congress had the power to elect the executive, he or she would answer to Congress, not the people of the nation. Direct election by the people was hardly even considered, however, because of the fear that a president with a great popular following might seize power and become a dictator. A choice by state legislature, with each state having one vote, was considered, but

President Franklin Delano Roosevelt ran for and won an unprecedented fourth term.

the states with large populations were naturally opposed to this. It would give the small states as much say in presidential elections as large ones.

The system finally agreed upon was an indirect election by "electors" chosen especially for the purpose of selecting the president. Presidential electors are collectively (as a group) called the Electoral College. During the early years of the republic, the presidential electors were, like senators, chosen by state legislatures rather than by a vote of the people.

There are as many electors from each state as the state has senators and representatives in Congress. This body of carefully chosen and highly educated men, in the Framers' vision, would calmly and deliberately choose the president according to their best judgment. This manner of election was designed to keep the country free from the dangers of political excitement and party strife.

The Electoral College system, however, docs not work exactly as it was planned. Political parties (which were feared as undemocratic when the Constitution was first written) nominate presidential candidates, and the electors exercise little, if any, independent judgment. The office of elector is purely honorary. If an elector did not vote for the candidate nominated by his or her party convention, he or she would be considered a traitor to the party.

Over the years, electors have been chosen in three ways: by the state legislatures, by the voters of the states voting by districts, and by the voters of the states voting on a general ticket. Today, electors are selected in every state on a general, or party, ticket. The system remains a complex and sometimes confusing one.

The rise of political parties has taken away the power of the Electoral College as a real method of voting for president. Since 1796, the electors have basically been "puppets" who have, for the most part, cast their ballots for the presidential candidate of the majority party in each state. That is, the electors vote for the candidate who received more votes in the state they represent than all other candidates, since only that candidate is entitled to the state's electoral votes.

Section 1: Election of President and Vice President

In the original Constitution, each elector had two votes, both technically for president. The candidate with the highest number of votes became president and the next highest became vice president. If there was not a majority, the election passed into the House of Representatives. The House, voting by state with each state having one vote, would choose from the five candidates with the highest number of votes. The Framers expected that the House would frequently have to elect the president. They assumed that electors would vote for prominent politicians from their own states or regions. Because in 1787 the United States lacked rapid means of communication such as telegraph, telephones, or the Internet, and because state loyalty was much stronger than loyalty to the nation, the Framers felt it would be very difficult for any one candidate to win a majority of the total electoral vote. In reality, however, the House has elected the president only twice: in 1800, when it elected Thomas Jefferson, and in 1824, when it elected John Quincy Adams.

John Quincy Adams, son of second President John Adams, was elected president in 1824 through a vote in the House of Representatives.

The entire system of choosing the president changed with ratification of the Twelfth Amendment in 1804. This amendment allows electors to cast separate votes for the president and vice president. This new system led to fewer ties. It also removed the possibility that two candidates from opposing political parties might become president and vice president of the same administration.

Section 1: Time for Choosing Electors

The Constitution directed that the time for choosing the electors should be determined by Congress. This time is the first Tuesday following the first Monday in November. (If November begins on a Tuesday, the election would take place on the following Tuesday.) A presidential voting year is always an even-numbered year that is exactly divisible by four (such as 2000, 2004, 2008, etc.). The electors chosen by the people meet in their state capitals on the first Monday after the second Wednesday in December to cast their official ballots for president.

Over the years, fraud crept into national elections because elections were held on different days in different states. Wagonloads of people would travel over state lines to vote again in more than one state. Election fraud became so widespread that people demanded a special national election day. In response, in 1845, Congress made a law making the Tuesday after the first Monday in November the date for national elections throughout the United States. This date falls about thirty days before the date set for electors to assemble in order to cast their ballots for president and vice president. Tuesday was selected to permit voters to travel on Monday in order to reach their voting polls, because travel in the early years of the nation was difficult.

Section 1: Qualifications for President

The Constitution outlines the qualifications for a president. First on the list is that the president must be a natural born citizen. "Natural born citizen" means a person born in the United States. Presidents must be thirty-five years old and must have lived in the United States for at least fourteen years. The residence qualification has been interpreted to mean residence at any time during the candidate's life, not necessarily the fourteen years just before election to the presidency. President Herbert Hoover, for example, lived abroad for many years before 1920. Nevertheless, he was considered eligible for the presidency in 1928, received the Republican nomination, and won the office.

Section 1: Presidential Succession

In accordance with the provisions of this clause, Congress passed the Presidential Succession Law of 1886. This law provides that in case of the removal, death, resignation, or inability of both the president and the vice president to carry out the duties of their respective offices, the office of president shall be assumed by the members of the Cabinet in the order of the establishment of their respective departments.[1]

President Richard Nixon has been the only president to resign office. Eight presidents have died in office: William Henry Harrison, Zachary Taylor, Abraham Lincoln, James A. Garfield, William C. McKinley, Warren G. Harding, Franklin D. Roosevelt, and John F. Kennedy. In each case, the vice president succeeded to the presidency.

Who decides when a president is unable to carry out the duties of office? In 1919 and 1920, the United States was almost leaderless when President Woodrow Wilson had a stroke, yet failed to give others authority to act for him. The situation arose again, though in a less severe form, when President Dwight Eisenhower became ill in 1955 and again in 1956. Despite the obvious need for clarification of the issue, up to 1962, Congress failed to pass a law empowering an individual or group to decide when the vice president should take over the executive functions of the government. In 1967, the Twenty-fifth Amendment was ratified. It created a procedure through which Congress is notified in writing by the president, vice president, or members of the Cabinet that the president cannot handle the duties of office, and establishes a system ensuring that a qualified acting president is available.

Section 1: Presidential Salary

From 1789 to 1873, presidents received an annual salary of $25,000. In 1873, the amount was increased to $50,000. Since then, it has been raised several times. In 1949, it was set at $100,000, plus an expense allowance of $90,000, of which $50,000 was tax-free. In 1969, it was raised to $200,000. The president's salary today is $400,000 with an expense allowance of $50,000, both of which are taxable, as well as allowances for such needs as travel and paying staff members.[2] The president is provided with a residence, the White House, and money is provided for its up-keep. The president may redecorate the interior of the White House, and select the household workers, such as chef, butlers, chauffeur, maids, and gardeners.

The president's salary may not be raised to take

effect during his or her term of office. This provision prevents Congress from influencing the president's actions by promising to increase his or her salary as a reward for signing a certain bill. Nor can Congress threaten the president with a decrease in salary.

The president is not allowed to receive any sum from a state.

Each former president is entitled to receive annually for the remainder of his or her life an amount equal to the salary of the head of an executive department, presently $161,200. Former presidents are also entitled to $96,000 per year for office staff. They are also furnished with suitable office space and are granted the continued use of the franking privilege (free mailing) that they enjoyed in office. The widow or widower of a president is entitled to receive a pension of $20,000 per year if she or he gives up the right to any annuity (regular yearly payments, rather than a lump sum at one time) or pension under any other act of Congress and does not remarry before becoming sixty years of age.

The Secret Service is authorized to protect former presidents and their spouses during their lifetime. The children of a former president receive protection until they reach the age of sixteen.

The salary of the vice president is $186,300 with an expense allowance of $10,000, as well as an allowance to pay staff.[3] The vice president is provided with a residence.

Section 1: Presidential Oath

The inauguration ceremony at which a new president takes the oath of office takes place in front of the Capitol building. The day on which the president is inducted into office is known as Inauguration Day.

The oath which is set forth in the Constitution states: "I do solemnly swear (or affirm) that I will faithfully execute the Office of President of the United States, and will to the best of my Ability, preserve, protect and defend the Constitution of the United States."[4]

Following the oath, which is administered by the Chief Justice of the United States, the president usually delivers a speech. George Washington was inaugurated as the first president of the United States on April 30, 1789. In all elections after that, up to and including that of 1932, the successful candidate took that oath of office on the March 4 after the election. The Twentieth Amendment, adopted in 1933, made January 20 the new date for presidential inaugurations. This shortened the time between the election of a president and his or her induction into office by six weeks.

7

Powers of the President, Article II, Sections 2–4

Powers of the President

Section 2. The President shall be commander in chief of the Army and Navy of the United States, and of the militia of the several states, when called into the actual service of the United States; he may require the opinion, in writing, of the principal officer in each of the executive departments, upon any subject relating to the duties of their respective offices, and he shall have power to grant reprieves and pardons for offenses against the United States, except in cases of impeachment.

He shall have power, by and with the advice and consent of the Senate, to make treaties, provided two thirds of the Senators present concur; and he shall nominate, and by and with the advice and consent of the Senate, shall appoint ambassadors, other public ministers and consuls, judges of the Supreme Court, and all other officers of the United States, whose appointments are not herein otherwise provided for, and which shall be established by law: but the

Congress may by law vest the appointment of such inferior officers, as they think proper, in the President alone, in the courts of law, or in the heads of departments.

The President shall have power to fill up all vacancies that may happen during the recess of the Senate, by granting commissions which shall expire at the end of their next session.

Section 3. He shall from time to time give to the Congress information of the state of the union, and recommend to their consideration such measures as he shall judge necessary and expedient; he may, on extraordinary occasions, convene both Houses, or either of them, and in case of disagreement between them, with respect to the time of adjournment, he may adjourn them to such time as he shall think proper; he shall receive ambassadors and other public ministers; he shall take care that the laws be faithfully executed, and shall commission all the officers of the United States.

Section 4. The President, Vice President and all civil officers of the United States, shall be removed from office on impeachment for, and conviction of, treason, bribery, or other high crimes and misdemeanors.

Section 2: Powers of the President

The major powers given to the president of the United States by the Constitution are essentially those that the king of England also had. They include the power to conduct foreign affairs; to be Commander in Chief of the military forces; the right to appoint executive and judicial officers; the right to reprieve or pardon those accused or convicted of crimes; and the power to veto proposed legislation.

Section 2: Military Power

In peacetime, the president may order troops or ships of war to go anywhere whenever he or she chooses. The president may not be a member of the military. Therefore, the military is ultimately under civilian control.

In war, the president's powers are tremendous. Perhaps the most outstanding example is President Abraham Lincoln's Emancipation Proclamation, which was issued on Sept. 22, 1862; and became effective on January 1, 1863. A war measure designed to encourage the Southern states to come back to the Union, it declared that all slaves held in places he considered to be in rebellion against the federal government would be freed. This was the largest property confiscation by a suit in history.

Section 2: The Cabinet

The Cabinet (the president's formal advisors, who head the various departments) is only hinted at in the Constitution. The Constitution states that the president may require the opinion in writing of the principal officer of each of the executive departments. This clause naturally assumes that there must be such departments and such officers. Five departments (and Cabinet offices) were created during first President George Washington's administration: state, treasury, chief justice, war, and attorney general. As the need has arisen, Congress has established other offices. Today, the Cabinet consists of the heads of the departments of state, treasury, defense, justice, interior, agriculture, commerce, labor, health and human services, housing and urban development, transportation, energy, education, and veterans' affairs.

Cabinet meetings are held on stated days, and naturally, the president asks the officers for advice. He or

George Washington appointed men with differing political views to his Cabinet.

she need not follow this advice, however. The president always retains the ultimate executive power.

Section 2: Treaties

The treaty-making power is in the hands of the president, but the secretary of state (a member of the Cabinet and the advisor who deals with foreign affairs) usually conducts the negotiations. To put a treaty into force, the Senate must approve it by a two-thirds vote of all the members. But the Senate has nothing to do with the treaty negotiations. It can ratify, or refuse to ratify, only when a treaty is submitted by the president for approval. It may, however, suggest amendments. In this case, the president may take the issue up again with the foreign power or powers involved, or let the whole matter drop, if there seems to be no possibility that the two-thirds approving vote will come from the Senate.

The outstanding example in American history of a treaty that was submitted by a president and rejected by the Senate is the Treaty of Versailles. This treaty was an agreement with defeated Germany and the other central powers at the end of World War I. Even though President Woodrow Wilson was active in creating the treaty, the Senate refused to ratify it, largely because it involved membership in the League of Nations, another of Wilson's ideas. The League would, like the modern United Nations, try to prevent wars through diplomacy. Ultimately, the Senate rejected the treaty, and the United States never became part of Wilson's vision for the League of Nations, which eventually failed.

Section 2: Appointments

Officers of the United States are appointed by the president with the advice and consent of the Senate, by the president alone, by the heads of departments, or by the courts of law. Before 1883, government positions were usually given to members of the party that won the election. In 1883, the Civil Service Commission was established when Congress passed the Pendleton Act. Under this law, the president was

President Woodrow Wilson helped to create the Treaty of Versailles, but Congress refused to ratify it.

authorized to place certain government positions on a classified list.[1] Since that time, thousands of positions have been added to this list.

The Constitution does not say anything, however, about the president's power to remove officers. Until 1867, the president removed people at will. Then, the Tenure of Office Act was passed, which made it necessary for the president to get the consent of the Senate before removing an officehold-er.[2] This law contrasted with common practice and was probably unconstitutional. It was repealed in 1887.

Section 2: Recess Appointments

In case of vacancy in an office when the Senate is on recess (not in session to approve a presidential appointment), to prevent the work of that office from suffering, the president may make a temporary, or recess, appointment. Usually, the name of a recess appointee is sent to the Senate for confirmation for a full term as soon as Congress assembles.

Section 3: Presidential Messages

The Constitution states that the president shall "from time to time give to the Congress Information of the State of the Union, and recommend to their

Consideration such Measures as he shall judge necessary and expedient." This clause provides the authority for the president's messages to Congress, such as the State of the Union Address or recommendations on legislation. Both George Washington and John Adams read their messages directly to Congress, but all subsequent presidents sent written messages until Woodrow Wilson revived the custom of appearing before Congress in person.

Presidents always send messages at the opening of each session of Congress. They may also send special messages whenever they think it is necessary. When emergencies arise, the president may call special sessions of Congress. The House is never called without the Senate, although the president may at times call the Senate without the House, to ratify treaties or confirm appointments.

The president's annual State of the Union message is considered a summary of the basic goals of the administration. The first message sent by a new president is especially significant. It generally covers a wide range of issues, highlighting the new president's intentions for the next four years.

Section 4: Impeachment

Section 4 of Article II describes the impeachment process by which the president and other executive officers of the federal government can be formally accused of crimes. If convicted by the Senate, the president or officer can be removed from office.

Since 1789, thirteen federal officials have been impeached. Four were found guilty by the Senate and removed from office; and one (Richard Nixon) resigned before the trial could be held.

The most famous case of impeachment in

Andrew Johnson was the first president to be impeached, in 1867, after Congress accused him of violating the Tenure of Office Act.

American history occurred in 1868, when President Andrew Johnson was impeached for violating the Tenure of Office Act (later repealed—1877). The President was acquitted by the margin of one vote short of the two-thirds necessary for conviction. The whole proceedings were prompted by bitter partisanship (party politics).

8

The Judicial Branch, Article III

The Judicial Branch

Section 1. The judicial power of the United States, shall be vested in one Supreme Court, and in such inferior courts as the Congress may from time to time ordain and establish. The judges, both of the supreme and inferior courts, shall hold their offices during good behavior, and shall, at stated times, receive for their services, a compensation, which shall not be diminished during their continuance in office.

Section 2. The judicial power shall extend to all cases, in law and equity, arising under this Constitution, the laws of the United States, and treaties made, or which shall be made, under their authority; to all cases affecting ambassadors, other public ministers and consuls; to all cases of admiralty and maritime jurisdiction; to controversies to which the United States shall be a party; to controversies between two or more states; between a state and citizens of another state; between citizens of different states; between citizens of the same state claiming lands under grants of different states, and between a state, or the citizens thereof, and foreign states, citizens or subjects.

In all cases affecting ambassadors, other public ministers and consuls, and those in which a state shall be party, the Supreme Court shall have original jurisdiction. In all the other cases before mentioned, the Supreme Court shall have appellate jurisdiction, both as to law and fact, with such exceptions, and under such regulations as the Congress shall make.

The trial of all crimes, except in cases of impeachment, shall be by jury; and such trial shall be held in the state where the said crimes shall have been committed; but when not committed within any state, the trial shall be at such place or places as the Congress may by law have directed.

Section 3. Treason against the United States, shall consist only in levying war against them, or in adhering to their enemies, giving them aid and comfort. No person shall be convicted of treason unless on the testimony of two witnesses to the same overt act, or on confession in open court.

The Congress shall have power to declare the punishment of treason, but no attainder of treason shall work corruption of blood, or forfeiture except during the life of the person attainted.

The Judicial Branch

The judiciary (court system) forms the third branch of the American federal government. Its structure, powers, and duties are outlined in Article III of the Constitution.

Section 1: Federal Courts

Congress has created thirteen "circuit" courts of appeals. The circuit courts have jurisdiction (authority) over almost all civil cases of federal notice—cases in which the citizenship of the parties involved or the nature of the dispute make them a federal concern.

There are also nearly one hundred district courts, with several hundred judges. These first district courts were created by Congress in 1789. They have original jurisdiction over most federal cases. There is at least one district court for every state, including Washington, D.C.

These courts may have from one to twenty-eight judges (appointed by the president and confirmed by the Senate). Judges serve for a period of "good behavior." A very small number have been impeached and convicted for committing crimes while in office.

Each district court is also assigned a United States district attorney. He or she is employed by the Department of Justice and not a court official. This person serves as the prosecuting attorney (District Attorney, or DA). The DA is a political appointee, and serves a four-year term.

Section 1: Other Courts

Under the authority derived (obtained) from its powers in Article I, Section 8, of the Constitution, Congress has also created other courts such as the Court of Federal Claims, Court of Appeals for the Armed Forces, and Court of Appeals for Veterans Affairs.

In the early days of the nation, it was impossible to bring suit against the federal government. It is partly for this reason that the Court of Claims was established in 1855. This court hears cases involving breaking contracts where the federal government is concerned.

Territorial courts serve the same purpose as District Courts, but they deal with the territories of the United States, and also handle some local matters. There are three of these courts, Guam, Virgin Islands, and Puerto Rico. In these courts (except in Puerto Rico where they are appointed for a term of "good behavior), the judges serve eight-year terms. Decisions may be appealed to the United States Courts of Appeal.

Any of these lower courts that have been created by Congress since the adoption of the Constitution can be abolished by an act of Congress, except the Supreme

The Supreme Court is responsible for determining if laws passed by Congress are in keeping with the provision of the Constitution.

Court, which is specifically provided for in the Constitution.

An ordinary federal case starts in the United States District Court. If its decision is appealed, it goes to a Court of Appeals. If a decision of this court is appealed, the case goes to the United States Supreme Court, whose decision is final.

The Supreme Court meets on the first Monday in October for a session that generally extends to the end of June. The sessions, which begin at 10 A.M., last until 3:00 P.M. They are open to the public Monday through Thursday. On Friday, the justices assemble for a private weekly conference. It is at these meetings that they discuss and vote on the cases that have been presented to them. They also vote on whether or not to hear cases that have been submitted.

Section 1: Federal Judges

Federal judges are appointed by the president with the advice and consent of the Senate. A judge's term lasts for good behavior, which usually means for life. The only way to remove a judge is by impeachment for inappropriate behavior.

The salary of a judge may be raised, but it cannot be lowered. This constitutional provision is designed to make the judiciary independent of Congress. In case Congress does not like the decisions of a certain judge, it cannot reduce the judge's salary as punishment, or try to change a judicial decision. Congress does have the power to determine the number of justices who sit on the Supreme Court.

Interestingly, the Constitution does not state what qualifications are demanded of federal judges. It mentions nothing about age, citizenship, legal competence, legal experience, education, or political

Chief Justice John Marshall helped formulate the doctrine of judicial review, which gave the Supreme Court the power to consider whether or not laws were valid under the Constitution.

viewpoints and background. However, the Senate Judiciary Committee, which has the right to accept or reject presidential appointments, demands high qualifications for judges.

Section 2: Jurisdiction of Federal Courts

In general, federal courts handle all cases arising under the Constitution, the laws of Congress, and treaties with foreign countries. In addition to federal courts, each state and the District of Columbia have court systems that are independent of the federal judiciary. There can be no appeal from the decision of the highest state courts to the federal courts, except on questions of federal law.

Under the Constitution, federal courts must handle admiralty and maritime matters. These would include all controversies involving United States registry ships upon the high seas and other navigable waters.

Courts of the United States inherited some types of law from England. Traditionally, the basic law was called "common law." It had its foundation in more than five hundred years of judicial decisions and custom. "Equity" was the special part of law that developed to cover instances where the common law did not apply, or to prevent an injustice from being done. The federal courts deal mostly in "statute law" (actual written laws) passed by Congress, treaties, or the Constitution.

Section 2: Judicial Review

Federal courts rule only on the specific cases that are brought before them. They never inform Congress that a proposed law will be unconstitutional if passed. When they decide a case, the courts' decisions are of great importance, because they serve as precedents (examples by which future cases will be decided).

The first sentence of Section 2, Clause 1, of Article III of the Constitution reads: "The judicial Power shall extend to all Cases, in Law and Equity, arising under this Constitution." Under this clause, the United States Supreme Court has the power of interpreting the laws of Congress. The Court has declared laws invalid (not legal) because they conflicted, in the opinion of the Court, with the Constitution, which is the supreme law of the land. As a result of this, the ability to have the final say on any law, the Supreme Court wields enormous power.

The act of checking whether laws are valid is called judicial review. The Supreme Court reviews the law, in cases brought before the court, to see if it conflicts with the Constitution. The power of the Supreme Court to declare acts of Congress and of the state legislatures unconstitutional is an implied power. That means it is not specifically granted but seemingly given to the Court by the wording of other powers given. This principle of judicial review, developed by John Marshall, chief justice of the Supreme Court, is considered the most distinctive feature of our constitutional system. Any court may rule on a question of constitutionality, but virtually all such questions involving congressional statutes or state laws reach the Supreme Court on appeal. This was done for the first time by Chief Justice Marshall in the 1803 case of Marbury v. Madison.[1]

Section 2: Jury Trial and Place of Trial

Clause 3 of Section 2 provides for a jury trial in cases of crimes against the United States. The United States grand jury indicts (makes formal charges) and a petit jury tries.

The petit jury usually consists of twelve persons. A unanimous vote is necessary to convict or acquit someone in federal court.

A person cannot be tried outside the state where the crime was committed. It is the general feeling that a person is more likely to receive justice if the case is placed in the hands of a jury living in the same community than if he or she is tried outside the home state. This provision also saves expense and trouble. It would be inconvenient and expensive to transport lawyers, court officials, and witnesses to a different state for a trial.

Section 3: Treason

In the early history of many countries, treason (acting as a traitor to the government) was vaguely defined or not defined at all. Therefore, whether a person would be found guilty of treason depended upon the judgment of those in power. To prevent this, the U.S. Constitution defines treason. A United States citizen can commit treason in only two ways: by waging war against the United States, or by helping an enemy when the country is at war or facing an internal rebellion. Evident intention to commit treason is not treason. Neither is sympathy for the enemy interpreted as treason. The Framers did not want anyone tried for treason merely for criticizing the government, as was done against Great Britain.

The Constitution safeguards a person accused of treason by requiring the testimony of at least two witnesses for conviction, unless the accused makes a confession in open court.

Perhaps the most famous treason trial in American

history involved Aaron Burr, the vice president of the United States under Thomas Jefferson. In 1807, Burr was charged with conspiracy against the government of the United States for trying to get parts of the nation to secede from the Union and form a new nation. Burr was acquitted because the prosecution was unable to prove that he was guilty of any overt act, and did not have two eyewitnesses.

Section 3: Punishment for Treason

Congress has the power to provide penalties for treason. However, no penalty may inflict punishment of any sort upon the innocent members of the guilty person's family, or deprive the heirs of their legal right to inherit the property of the guilty individual, or of any other legal right.

9

Interstate Relations, Article IV

Relations of the States to Each Other

Section 1. Full faith and credit shall be given in each state to the public acts, records, and judicial proceedings of every other state. And the Congress may by general laws prescribe the manner in which such acts, records, and proceedings shall be proved, and the effect thereof.

Section 2. The citizens of each state shall be entitled to all privileges and immunities of citizens in the several states.

A person charged in any state with treason, felony, or other crime, who shall flee from justice, and be found in another state, shall on demand of the executive authority of the state from which he fled, be delivered up, to be removed to the state having jurisdiction of the crime.

No person held to service or labor in one state, under the laws thereof, escaping into another, shall, in consequence of any law or regulation therein, be discharged from such service or labor, but shall be delivered up on claim of the party to whom such ser-vice or labor may be due.

Federal-State Relations

Section 3. New states may be admitted by the Congress into this union; but no new states shall be formed or erected within the jurisdiction of any other state; nor any state be formed by the junction of two or more states, or parts of states, without the consent of the legislatures of the states concerned as well as of the Congress.

The Congress shall have power to dispose of and make all needful rules and regulations respecting the terri-tory or other property belonging to the United States; and nothing in this Constitution shall be so construed as to prejudice any claims of the United States, or of any particular state.

Section 4. The United States shall guarantee to every state in this union a republican form of government, and shall protect each of them against invasion; and on application of the legislature, or of the executive (when the legislature cannot be convened) against domestic violence.

Article IV: Interstate Relations

Under the Constitution, the states composing the Union all have equal status. Therefore, the laws, judi-cial proceedings, and legal records of any one state must be held in good faith (accepted) by every other state.

Section 1: Official Acts

The public acts of a state are its enacted (passed) laws, those that have been duly passed, approved, written, and recorded. If a will is allowed by a probate court in a state, then the terms of this must be accepted in every state where someone who is interested in the will lives. By the same token, if a deed is properly recorded in the registration office of one state, the courts of every state are bound to recognize this registration.

This provision, however, does not extend to many matters that fall within what is called the "police power" of the states. For instance, licenses to practice medicine, law, engineering, or teaching are not recognized in every state. States have the right to make their own requirements.

Section 2: Mutual Duties of States

The Constitution provides that "The Citizens of each State shall be entitled to all Privileges and Immunities of Citizens in the several States." This allows citizens of the United States to travel freely from one state to another, and do business in all states. A person who goes from one state to another does not take along the privileges he or she enjoyed in his or her own state, but does automatically acquire the privileges of the citizens of the state into which he or she goes.

Section 2: Extradition

A person who is accused of committing a crime in one state may be turned over to the proper authorities of that state from another upon the request of the first state's governor. This procedure is known as rendition (extradition is a term that should be reserved for the international field, but is often used

interchangeably). When a person is accused of committing crimes in several states, he or she is generally
turned over to the state that charges him or her with
the most serious offense. Although the Constitution
explicitly directs that a fugitive shall be turned over to
the authorities of the state from which he or she has
fled, there are cases where governors have successfully
refused demands for rendition. If the governor refus-
es, there is no way to compel him or her to grant
rendition, because Congress has never passed any laws
on the subject.

Section 3, Clause 1: Admission of New States

A new state may be formed out of the territory of an
existing state only with the consent of the legislature
of that state. For example, Kentucky was separated
from Virginia in 1792, and Maine was separated from
Massachusetts and entered the Union in 1820. West
Virginia was separated from Virginia and admitted
into the Union in 1863 while Virginia was in rebellion
against the United States during the Civil War. Even
in this instance, however, federal authorities took care
to get the consent of those representatives of Virginia
who had remained loyal to the Union.

In general, the following process is pursued in
admitting new states: A constitutional convention is
held in a territory, and a constitution is drafted. The
territory then applies for admission into the Union as
a state. If a majority of Congress approves the territory's constitution, it may vote to admit the territory as
a state. If a majority of Congress disapproves the proposed state constitution, no power can force Congress
to admit this territory as a state. If the people of the

President Thomas Jefferson bought the Louisiana Territory from French Emperor Napoleon Bonaparte (seen here).

territory change the constitution to meet the views of the majority in Congress, Congress may vote again.

When Louisiana was admitted to the Union in 1812, there was an objection raised in the eastern states to giving people so far away an equal voice in the government. The policy prevailed, and since that time, state after state has been admitted on terms of exact equality with the thirteen original states.

There does not exist anywhere in the Constitution a statement or reference that the federal government has the right to acquire new territory by conquest, purchase, or treaty agreements. This fact proved embarrassing for President Thomas Jefferson, a strict constructionist, who believed the government could do only what was explicitly stated in the Constitution. In 1803, Jefferson had the opportunity to buy the vast Louisiana Territory from France. Jefferson was persuaded by advisors to make the purchase while he had the chance. He bought it in 1803 for $15 million. Although some people claimed that the sale was unconstitutional, the rest of the government eventually accepted the purchase. It turned out to be one of America's greatest real estate bargains.

Section 3, Clause 2: Control over Territory and Property

United States territories are governed by laws passed by Congress. The government consists of a governor and judges appointed by the president, as well as a territorial legislature elected by the people of the territory. The territory sends a nonvoting delegate to Congress. This delegate may speak on matters affecting the territory, but does not have the right to vote.

At the time of the writing of the Constitution, the national government held large areas of western lands. In the very year the Constitution was framed, the Confederation Congress adopted the Ordinance of 1787, which regulated the administration of what was then called the Northwest Territory. This served as a model for the organization of all other continental territories. It established the principle of self-government and ultimate admission to statehood.

Section 4: Federal Protection for States

A "republican form of government" is usually understood as any type of representative democracy, one in which people elect their officials at certain intervals. If any person or persons try to set themselves up as tyrants in a state, it is the duty of the federal government to intervene.

The federal government must also protect the individual states from invasion. Under this provision, the United States government might decide to intervene if a state attempted to set up a dictatorship.

The states, in most instances, are expected to take care of cases of domestic uprisings themselves. But if circumstances are such that a disturbance in a state goes beyond control of the state authorities, the state legislature or governor may ask for federal aid. If a disturbance in a state gets so big or out of control that the functions of the federal government are hindered, the president may order federal troops to quell (put down) the disturbance without waiting for requests from the state authorities. This action was taken by President Grover Cleveland in 1894 in connection with the Pullman strike in Chicago. This railroad workers strike eventually spread to affect railroad service all over the nation. Cleveland decided he had to stop the strike to restore order across the United States. The government intervention, which ended in violence, hurt the labor movement, which did not recover until well into the twentieth century.

10

The Amending Process, Article V

Amending the Constitution

The Congress, whenever two thirds of both houses shall deem it necessary, shall propose amendments to this Constitution, or, on the application of the legislatures of two thirds of the several states, shall call a convention for proposing amendments, which, in either case, shall be valid to all intents and purposes, as part of this Constitution, when ratified by the legislatures of three fourths of the several states, or by conventions in three fourths thereof, as the one or the other mode of ratification may be proposed by the Congress; provided that no amendment which may be made prior to the year one thousand eight hundred and eight shall in any manner affect the first and fourth clauses in the ninth section of the first article; and that no state, without its consent, shall be deprived of its equal suffrage in the Senate.

The Amending Process

During the Confederation period (1776–1787), it was almost impossible to amend the Articles of Confederation, because the consent of all the states

Prohibition made intoxicating liquors illegal. Some people found ways to drink, however, in places called speakeasies.

was needed. This problem was one of the many reasons the Framers wanted to create a new Constitution.

The amending process under the United States
Constitution, although cumbersome, has proved
far more workable than that of the Articles of
Confederation. Amendments to the federal
Constitution may be formally proposed by any of the
following methods: by a two-thirds vote of both houses of Congress; by a national convention called by
Congress (when at least two thirds of the states have
requested one); by the legislatures of three-fourths of
the states; or by a special convention held in at least
three-fourths of the states.

The most common way to amend the Constitution
is for Congress to pass the proposed amendment by a
two-thirds vote in each of the houses. The proposed
amendment then goes to the state legislatures for ratification. It becomes a valid part of the Constitution
only after it has been ratified by three fourths of the
legislatures of the states. All constitutional amendments but one up to the present time have been made
in this manner. The Twenty-first Amendment, which
ended Prohibition (making intoxicating liquors
illegal), was made by state conventions. Congress
decides if ratification of a proposed amendment shall
be by state legislatures or conventions.

Federal Credit and Federal Supremacy, Article VI

11

National Debt

All debts contracted and engagements entered into, before the adoption of this Constitution, shall be as valid against the United States under this Constitution, as under the Confederation.

Supremacy of the National Government

This Constitution, and the laws of the United States which shall be made in pursuance thereof; and all treaties made, or which shall be made, under the authority of the United States, shall be the supreme law of the land; and the judges in every state shall be bound thereby, anything in the Constitution or laws of any State to the contrary notwithstanding.

The Senators and Representatives before mentioned, and the members of the several state legislatures, and all executive and judicial officers, both of the United States and of the several states, shall be bound by oath or affirmation, to support this Constitution; but no religious test shall ever be required as a qualification to any office or public trust under the United States.

Federal Credit and Federal Supremacy

Before the new Constitution would be accepted by all the states, the Framers knew they had to make sure the provisions would make people's lives better in the difficult years after the end of the American Revolution. This was especially true for the business community of the northeastern states. These people were sure to worry about how the new Constitution would affect them financially.

Public Debt of the United States

The new government, as part of the Constitution, promised to honor the obligations and contracts that came about under the Articles of Confederation. This provision was added to make sure the Constitution would win the support of the merchant and financial classes to whom contracts were important for business.

Some of future Secretary of the Treasury Alexander Hamilton's financial policies, such as the funding of the domestic and foreign debts of the national government and the assumption of state debts from the Revolution, were based largely on this clause. Hamilton funded domestic and foreign debts by selling government bonds. Hamilton offered bonds at a higher interest rate than the old ones being turned in. Hamilton also believed that the federal government should take over the debts made by the states during the Revolution. He argued that the war had been a national effort. All the states had shared in fighting and paying for the war to create a new nation. Hamilton believed it was the responsibility of the newly formed government to take over the debt payments of the individual states.

Alexander Hamilton was a brilliant secretary of the treasury, who helped the young United States start a stable economy that would be respected by other nations of the world.

The Supreme Law of the Land

Article VI, Section 2 is known as the Supreme Law of the Land Clause. It establishes the supremacy of the federal government over the state governments, and the Constitution and laws made by Congress over the laws made by the state legislatures where the federal government has jurisdiction.

All judges, not only in the federal courts, but also in the state courts, are bound by the United States Constitution, United States laws, and treaties, even if the constitution or laws of any individual state are in conflict with the federal laws.

Below the Constitution, in order of descending (most important to least important) authority, are: federal laws, treaties, state constitutions, state laws, and local laws or statutes.

Official Oath, No Religious Test

Not only must the president and state and federal judges swear to support the Constitution of the United States, but state senators and representatives as well as United States senators and representatives, must be bound by the oath of affirmation. To establish the supremacy of the Constitution and the federal government even more firmly, all executive and judicial officers (both of the United States and of the states) are bound by oath or affirmation to support the United States Constitution. This required oath makes all civil officials (from police officers to governors) agents of the federal government.

The Constitution, though stringent in demanding that officers swear to uphold its provisions, is clear in stating that no religious test may be required of an officer. This demand emphasizes the secular (free from religious influences) character of the American government, which is reinforced by the First Amendment. The clauses of the Constitution establishing a secular government, however, did not apply to the states.

12

Ratification, Article VII

Ratifying the Constitution

The ratification of the conventions of nine states, shall be sufficient for the establishment of this Constitution between the states so ratifying the same.

Done in convention by the unanimous consent of the states present the seventeenth day of September in the year of our Lord one thousand seven hundred and eighty seven and of the independence of the United States of America the twelfth. In witness whereof We have hereunto subscribed our Names,

✎ Ratification

The final article of the United States Constitution outlines the process by which it would become the formal governing instrument of the nation.

Following this are listed the names of those delegates to the Constitutional Convention who accepted and signed the final document: President of the Convention and delegate from Virginia George Washington; John Langdon and Nicholas Gilman

Benjamin Franklin of Pennsylvania was the oldest delegate to the Constitutional Convention, as well as one of the most famous.

from New Hampshire; Rufus King and Nathaniel Gorham from Massachusetts; William Samuel Johnson and Roger Sherman from Connecticut; Alexander Hamilton from New York; David Brearley, Jonathan Dayton, William Paterson, and William Livingston from New Jersey; Thomas Mifflin, Thomas FitzSimons, Robert Norris, James Wilson, George Clymer, Gouverneur Morris, Jared Ingersoll, and Benjamin Franklin from Pennsylvania; George Read, Richard Bassett, Gunning Bedford, Jr., Jacob Broom, and John Dickinson from Delaware; James McHenry, Daniel of St. Thomas Jenifer, and Daniel Carroll from Maryland; John Blair and James Madison, Jr., from Virginia; Richard Dobbs Spaight, William Blount, and Hugh Williamson from North Carolina; John Rutledge, Charles Pinckney, Charles Cotesworth Pinckney, and Pierce Butler from South Carolina; and William Few and Abraham Baldwin from Georgia. Also signing the final document, to testify to the fact that each of the listed delegates did, in fact, sign the Constitution, was William Jackson, secretary of the Convention.

The Constitution was then sent to the states, and the battle to win approval, which was eventually won, began.

13

Legacy

Although the United States Constitution has changed somewhat through amendments and through interpretation in the years since it was adopted in 1789, the major system established by its Articles has remained the same. The Articles of the Constitution surpassed even the Framers' greatest hopes, creating an effective government that has transferred power from one presidential administration to the next without violence or serious friction, (with the exception, of course, of the Civil War), for over two centuries. The Articles of the Constitution have kept the United States government working smoothly almost always, even through terrible crises that included a bloody Civil War, two world wars, and the Great Depression.

As certain minorities, such as African Americans and women, began to demand to be treated as equal citizens, the Articles and the amendment process have allowed the Constitution to expand to include these individuals. The amendment process has also made America a more direct democracy, allowing the people to elect senators directly and making the Electoral College confirm the vote of the people. All of these changes have been made, thanks to the extraordinary provisions of the Constitution. Over the years, the Constitution has stood the test of time. It promises to continue to protect the rights of American citizens and to provide an orderly government.

African Americans and other minorities used their many freedoms under the Constitution to demand changes in the way they were treated.

THE CONSTITUTION OF THE UNITED STATES

The text of the Constitution is presented here. All words are given their modern spelling and capitalization. Brackets [ ] indicate parts that have been changed or set aside by amendments.

Preamble

We the People of the United States, in Order to form a more perfect Union, establish Justice, insure domestic Tranquillity, provide for the common defence, promote the general Welfare, and secure the Blessings of Liberty to ourselves and our Posterity, do ordain and establish this Constitution for the United States of America.

ARTICLE I

The Legislative Branch

Section 1. All legislative powers herein granted shall be vested in a Congress of the United States, which shall consist of a Senate and House of Representatives.

The House of Representatives

Section 2. (1) The House of Representatives shall be composed of members chosen every second year by the people of the several states, and the electors in each state shall have the qualifications requisite for electors of the most numerous branch of the state legislature.

(2) No person shall be a Representative who shall not have attained to the age of twenty five years, and been seven years a citizen of the United States, and who shall not, when elected, be an inhabitant of that state in which he shall be chosen.

(3) Representatives and direct taxes shall be apportioned among the several states which may be included within this union, according to their respective numbers, [which shall be determined by adding to the whole number of free persons, including those bound to service for a term of years, and excluding Indians not taxed, three fifths of all other persons]. The actual Enumeration shall be made within three years after the first meeting of the Congress of the United States, and within every subsequent term of ten years, in such manner as they shall by law direct. The number of Representatives shall not exceed one for every thirty thousand, but each state shall have at least one Representative; [and until such enumeration shall be made, the state of New Hampshire shall be entitled to chuse three, Massachusetts eight, Rhode Island and Providence Plantations one, Connecticut five, New York six, New Jersey four, Pennsylvania eight, Delaware one, Maryland six, Virginia ten, North Carolina five, South Carolina five, and Georgia three].

(4) When vacancies happen in the Representation from any state, the executive authority thereof shall issue writs of election to fill such vacancies.

(5) The House of Representatives shall choose their speaker and other officers; and shall have the sole power of impeachment.

The Senate

Section 3. (1) The Senate of the United States shall be composed of two Senators from each state, [chosen by the legislature thereof,] for six years; and each Senator shall have one vote.

(2) Immediately after they shall be assembled in consequence of the first election, they shall be divided as equally as may be into three classes. The seats of the Senators of the first class shall be vacated at the expiration of the second year, of the second class at the expiration of the fourth year, and the third class at the expiration of the sixth year, so that one third may be chosen every second year; [and if vacancies happen by resignation, or otherwise, during the recess of the legislature of any state, the executive thereof may make temporary appointments until the next meeting of the legislature, which shall then fill such vacancies].

(3) No person shall be a Senator who shall not have attained to the age of thirty years, and been nine years a citizen of the United States and who shall not, when elected, be an inhabitant of that state for which he shall be chosen.

(4) The Vice President of the United States shall be President of the Senate, but shall have no vote, unless they be equally divided.

(5)The Senate shall choose their other officers, and also a President *pro tempore,* in the absence of the Vice President, or when he shall exercise the office of President of the United States.

(6) The Senate shall have the sole power to try all impeachments. When sitting for that purpose, they shall

be on oath or affirmation. When the President of the
United States is tried, the Chief Justice shall preside: And
no person shall be convicted without the concurrence of
two thirds of the members present.

(7) Judgment in cases of impeachment shall not extend
further than to removal from office, and disqualification to
hold and enjoy any office of honor, trust or profit under
the United States: but the party convicted shall nevertheless be liable and subject to indictment, trial, judgment
and punishment, according to law.

Organization of Congress

Section 4. (1) The times, places and manner of holding
elections for Senators and Representatives, shall be prescribed in each state by the legislature thereof; but the
Congress may at any time by law make or alter such regulations, [except as to the places of choosing Senators].

(2) The Congress shall assemble at least once in every year,
[and such meeting shall be on the first Monday in
December], unless they shall by law appoint a different
day.

Section 5. (1) Each House shall be the judge of the elections, returns and qualifications of its own members, and
a majority of each shall constitute a quorum to do business; but a smaller number may adjourn from day to day,
and may be authorized to compel the attendance of absent
members, in such manner, and under such penalties as
each House may provide.

(2) Each House may determine the rules of its proceedings, punish its members for disorderly behavior, and, with the concurrence of two thirds, expel a member.

(3) Each House shall keep a journal of its proceedings, and from time to time publish the same, excepting such parts as may in their judgment require secrecy; and the yeas and nays of the members of either House on any question shall, at the desire of one fifth of those present, be entered on the journal.

(4) Neither House, during the session of Congress, shall, without the consent of the other, adjourn for more than three days, nor to any other place than that in which the two Houses shall be sitting.

Section 6. (1) The Senators and Representatives shall receive a compensation for their services, to be ascertained by law, and paid out of the treasury of the United States. They shall in all cases, except treason, felony and breach of the peace, be privileged from arrest during their attendance at the session of their respective Houses, and in going to and returning from the same; and for any speech or debate in either House, they shall not be questioned in any other place.

(2) No Senator or Representative shall, during the time for which he was elected, be appointed to any civil office under the authority of the United States, which shall have been created, or the emoluments whereof shall have been increased during such time: and no person holding any office under the United States, shall be a member of either House during his continuance in office.

Section 7. (1) All bills for raising revenue shall originate in the House of Representatives; but the Senate may propose or concur with amendments as on other Bills.

(2) Every bill which shall have passed the House of Representatives and the Senate, shall, before it become a law, be presented to the President of the United States; if he approve he shall sign it, but if not he shall return it, with his objections to that House in which it shall have originated, who shall enter the objections at large on their journal, and proceed to reconsider it. If after such reconsideration two thirds of that House shall agree to pass the bill, it shall be sent, together with the objections, to the other House, by which it shall likewise be reconsidered, and if approved by two thirds of that House, it shall become a law. But in all such cases the votes of both Houses shall be determined by yeas and nays, and the names of the persons voting for and against the bill shall be entered on the journal of each House respectively. If any bill shall not be returned by the President within ten days (Sundays excepted) after it shall have been presented to him, the same shall be a law, in like manner as if he had signed it, unless the Congress by their adjournment prevent its return, in which case it shall not be a law.

(3) Every order, resolution, or vote to which the concurrence of the Senate and House of Representatives may be necessary (except on a question of adjournment) shall be presented to the President of the United States; and before the same shall take effect, shall be approved by him, or being disapproved by him, shall be repassed by two thirds of the Senate and House of Representatives, according to the rules and limitations prescribed in the case of a bill.

Powers Granted to Congress
The Congress shall have the power:

Section 8. (1) To lay and collect taxes, duties, imposts and excises, to pay the debts and provide for the common defense and general welfare of the United States; but all duties, imposts and excises shall be uniform throughout the United States;

(2) To borrow money on the credit of the United States;

(3) To regulate commerce with foreign nations, and among the several states, and with the Indian tribes;

(4) To establish a uniform rule of naturalization, and uniform laws on the subject of bankruptcies throughout the United States;

(5) To coin money, regulate the value thereof, and of foreign coin, and fix the standard of weights and measures;

(6) To provide for the punishment of counterfeiting the securities and current coin of the United States;

(7) To establish post offices and post roads;

(8) To promote the progress of science and useful arts, by securing for limited times to authors and inventors the exclusive right to their respective writings and discoveries;

(9) To constitute tribunals inferior to the Supreme Court;

(10) To define and punish piracies and felonies committed on the high seas, and offenses against the law of nations;

(11) To declare war, grant letters of marque and reprisal, and make rules concerning captures on land and water;

(12) To raise and support armies, but no appropriation of money to that use shall be for a longer term than two years;

(13) To provide and maintain a navy;

(14) To make rules for the government and regulation of the land and naval forces;

(15) To provide for calling forth the militia to execute the laws of the union, suppress insurrections and repel invasions;

(16) To provide for organizing, arming, and disciplining, the militia, and for governing such part of them as may be employed in the service of the United States, reserving to the states respectively, the appointment of the officers, and the authority of training the militia according to the discipline prescribed by Congress;

(17) To exercise exclusive legislation in all cases whatsoever, over such District (not exceeding ten miles square) as may, by cession of particular states, and the acceptance of Congress, become the seat of the government of the United States, and to exercise like authority over all places purchased by the consent of the legislature of the state in which the same shall be, for the erection of forts, magazines, arsenals, dockyards, and other needful buildings;—And

(18) To make all laws which shall be necessary and proper for carrying into execution the foregoing powers, and all

other powers vested by this Constitution in the government of the United States, or in any department or officer thereof.

Powers Forbidden to Congress

Section 9. (1) The migration or importation of such persons as any of the states now existing shall think proper to admit, shall not be prohibited by the Congress prior to the year one thousand eight hundred and eight, but a tax or duty may be imposed on such importation, not exceeding ten dollars for each person.

(2) The privilege of the writ of *habeas corpus* shall not be suspended, unless when in cases of rebellion or invasion the public safety may require it.

(3) No bill of attainder or *ex post facto* Law shall be passed.

(4) No capitation, [or other direct,] tax shall be laid, unless in proportion to the census or enumeration herein before directed to be taken.

(5) No tax or duty shall be laid on articles exported from any state.

(6) No preference shall be given by any regulation of commerce or revenue to the ports of one state over those of another: nor shall vessels bound to, or from, one state, be obliged to enter, clear or pay duties in another.

(7) No money shall be drawn from the treasury, but in consequence of appropriations made by law; and a regular statement and account of receipts and expenditures of all public money shall be published from time to time.

(8) No title of nobility shall be granted by the United States: and no person holding any office of profit or trust under them, shall, without the consent of the Congress, accept of any present, emolument, office, or title, of any kind whatever, from any king, prince, or foreign state.

Powers Forbidden to the States

Section 10. (1) No state shall enter into any treaty, alliance, or confederation; grant letters of marque and reprisal; coin money; emit bills of credit; make anything but gold and silver coin a tender in payment of debts; pass any bill of attainder, *ex post facto* law, or law impairing the obligation of contracts, or grant any title of nobility.

(2) No state shall, without the consent of the Congress, lay any imposts or duties on imports or exports, except what may be absolutely necessary for executing its inspection laws: and the net produce of all duties and imposts, laid by any state on imports or exports, shall be for the use of the treasury of the United States; and all such laws shall be subject to the revision and control of the Congress.

(3) No state shall, without the consent of Congress, lay any duty of tonnage, keep troops, or ships of war in time of peace, enter into any agreement or compact with another state, or with a foreign power, or engage in war, unless actually invaded, or in such imminent danger as will not admit of delay.

ARTICLE II

The Executive Branch

Section 1. (1) The executive power shall be vested in a President of the United States of America. He shall hold his office during the term of four years, and, together with the Vice President, chosen for the same term, be elected, as follows:

(2) Each state shall appoint, in such manner as the Legislature thereof may direct, a number of electors, equal to the whole number of Senators and Representatives to which the State may be entitled in the Congress: but no Senator or Representative, or person holding an office of trust or profit under the United States, shall be appointed an elector.

(3) [The electors shall meet in their respective states, and vote by ballot for two persons, of whom one at least shall not be an inhabitant of the same state with themselves. And they shall make a list of all the persons voted for, and of the number of votes for each; which list they shall sign and certify, and transmit sealed to the seat of the government of the United States, directed to the President of the Senate. The President of the Senate shall, in the presence of the Senate and House of Representatives, open all the certificates, and the votes shall then be counted. The person having the greatest number of votes shall be the President, if such number be a majority of the whole number of electors appointed; and if there be more than one who have such majority, and have an equal number of votes, then the House of Representatives shall immediately choose by ballot one of them for President; and if no person have a majority, then from the five highest on the list the said House shall in like manner choose the President. But in choosing the President, the votes shall be taken by States, the representation from each state having one vote; A quorum for this purpose shall consist of a member or members from two thirds of the states, and a majority of all the states shall be necessary to a choice. In

every case, after the choice of the President, the person having the greatest number of votes of the electors shall be the Vice President. But if there should remain two or more who have equal votes, the Senate shall choose from them by ballot the Vice President.]

(4) The Congress may determine the time of choosing the electors, and the day on which they shall give their votes; which day shall be the same throughout the United States.

(5) No person except a natural born citizen, or a citizen of the United States, at the time of the adoption of this Constitution, shall be eligible to the office of President; neither shall any person be eligible to that office who shall not have attained to the age of thirty five years, and been fourteen Years a resident within the United States.

(6) In case of the removal of the President from office, or of his death, resignation, or inability to discharge the powers and duties of the said office, the same shall devolve on the Vice President, and the Congress may by law provide for the case of removal, death, resignation or inability, both of the President and Vice President, declaring what officer shall then act as President, and such officer shall act accordingly, until the disability be removed, or a President shall be elected.

(7) The President shall, at stated times, receive for his services, a compensation, which shall neither be increased nor diminished during the period for which he shall have been elected, and he shall not receive within that period any other emolument from the United States, or any of them.

(8) Before he enter on the execution of his office, he shall take the following oath or affirmation:—"I do solemnly

swear (or affirm) that I will faithfully execute the office of President of the United States, and will to the best of my ability, preserve, protect and defend the Constitution of the United States."

Section 2. (1) The President shall be commander in chief of the Army and Navy of the United States, and of the militia of the several states, when called into the actual service of the United States; he may require the opinion, in writing, of the principal officer in each of the executive departments, upon any subject relating to the duties of their respective offices, and he shall have power to grant reprieves and pardons for offenses against the United States, except in cases of impeachment.

(2) He shall have power, by and with the advice and consent of the Senate, to make treaties, provided two thirds of the Senators present concur; and he shall nominate, and by and with the advice and consent of the Senate, shall appoint ambassadors, other public ministers and consuls, judges of the Supreme Court, and all other officers of the United States, whose appointments are not herein otherwise provided for, and which shall be established by law: but the Congress may by law vest the appointment of such inferior officers, as they think proper, in the President alone, in the courts of law, or in the heads of departments.

(3) The President shall have power to fill up all vacancies that may happen during the recess of the Senate, by granting commissions which shall expire at the end of their next session.

Section 3. He shall from time to time give to the Congress information of the state of the union, and recommend to their consideration such measures as he shall judge necessary and expedient; he may, on extraordinary occasions, convene both Houses, or either of them, and in case of disagreement between them, with respect to the time of adjournment, he may adjourn them to such time as he shall think proper; he shall receive ambassadors and other public ministers; he shall take care that the laws be faithfully executed, and shall commission all the officers of the United States.

Section 4. The President, Vice President and all civil officers of the United States, shall be removed from office on impeachment for, and conviction of, treason, bribery, or other high crimes and misdemeanors.

ARTICLE III
The Judicial Branch

Section 1. The judicial power of the United States, shall be vested in one Supreme Court, and in such inferior courts as the Congress may from time to time ordain and establish. The judges, both of the supreme and inferior courts, shall hold their offices during good behaviour, and shall, at stated times, receive for their services, a compensation, which shall not be diminished during their continuance in office.

Section 2. (1) The judicial power shall extend to all cases, in law and equity, arising under this Constitution, the laws of the United States, and treaties made, or which shall be made, under their authority;—to all cases affecting ambassadors, other public ministers and consuls;—to all cases of admiralty and maritime jurisdiction;—to controversies to which the United States shall be a party;—to controversies between two or more states;[—between a state and citizens of another state;]— between citizens of different states;—between citizens of the same state claiming lands under grants of different states, and between a state, or the citizens thereof, and foreign states, [citizens or subjects].

(2) In all cases affecting ambassadors, other public ministers and consuls, and those in which a state shall be party, the Supreme Court shall have original jurisdiction. In all the other cases before mentioned, the Supreme Court shall have appellate jurisdiction, both as to law and fact, with such exceptions, and under such regulations as the Congress shall make.

(3) The trial of all crimes, except in cases of impeachment, shall be by jury; and such trial shall be held in the state where the said crimes shall have been committed; but when not committed within any state, the trial shall be at such place or places as the Congress may by law have directed.

Section 3. (1) Treason against the United States, shall consist only in levying war against them, or in adhering to their enemies, giving them aid and comfort. No person shall be convicted of treason unless on the testimony of two witnesses to the same overt act, or on confession in open court.

(2) The Congress shall have power to declare the punishment of treason, but no attainder of treason shall work corruption of blood, or forfeiture except during the life of the person attainted.

ARTICLE IV

Relation of the States to Each Other

Section 1. Full faith and credit shall be given in each state to the public acts, records, and judicial proceedings of every other state. And the Congress may by general laws prescribe the manner in which such acts, records, and proceedings shall be proved, and the effect thereof.

Section 2. (1) The citizens of each state shall be entitled to all privileges and immunities of citizens in the several states.

(2) A person charged in any state with treason, felony, or other crime, who shall flee from justice, and be found in another state, shall on demand of the executive authority of the state from which he fled, be delivered up, to be removed to the state having jurisdiction of the crime.

(3) [No person held to service or labor in one state, under the laws thereof, escaping into another, shall, in consequence of any law or regulation therein, be discharged from such service or labor, but shall be delivered up on claim of the party to whom such service or labor may be due.]

Federal-State Relations

Section 3. (1) New states may be admitted by the Congress into this union; but no new states shall be formed or erected within the jurisdiction of any other state; nor any state be formed by the junction of two or more states, or parts of states, without the consent of the legislatures of the states concerned as well as of the Congress.

(2) The Congress shall have power to dispose of and make all needful rules and regulations respecting the territory or

other property belonging to the United States; and nothing in this Constitution shall be so construed as to prejudice any claims of the United States, or of any particular state.

Section 4. The United States shall guarantee to every state in this union a republican form of government, and shall protect each of them against invasion; and on application of the legislature, or of the executive (when the legislature cannot be convened) against domestic violence.

ARTICLE V

Amending the Constitution

The Congress, whenever two thirds of both houses shall deem it necessary, shall propose amendments to this Constitution, or, on the application of the legislatures of two thirds of the several states, shall call a convention for proposing amendments, which, in either case, shall be valid to all intents and purposes, as part of this Constitution, when ratified by the legislatures of three fourths of the several states, or by conventions in three fourths thereof, as the one or the other mode of ratification may be proposed by the Congress; provided [that no amendment which may be made prior to the year one thousand eight hundred and eight shall in any manner affect the first and fourth clauses in the ninth section of the first article; and] that no state, without its consent, shall be deprived of its equal suffrage in the Senate.

ARTICLE VI

National Debts

(1) All debts contracted and engagements entered into, before the adoption of this Constitution, shall be as valid

against the United States under this Constitution, as under the Confederation.

Supremacy of the National Government

(2) This Constitution, and the laws of the United States which shall be made in pursuance thereof; and all treaties made, or which shall be made, under the authority of the United States, shall be the supreme law of the land; and the judges in every state shall be bound thereby, anything in the Constitution or laws of any State to the contrary notwithstanding.

(3) The Senators and Representatives before mentioned, and the members of the several state legislatures, and all executive and judicial officers, both of the United States and of the several states, shall be bound by oath or affirmation, to support this Constitution; but no religious test shall ever be required as a qualification to any office or public trust under the United States.

ARTICLE VII

Ratifying the Constitution

The ratification of the conventions of nine states, shall be sufficient for the establishment of this Constitution between the states so ratifying the same.

Done in convention by the unanimous consent of the states present the seventeenth day of September in the year of our Lord one thousand seven hundred and eighty seven and of the independence of the United States of

America the twelfth. In witness whereof We have hereunto subscribed our Names.

Amendments to the Constitution

The first ten amendments, known as the Bill of Rights, were proposed on September 25, 1789. They were ratified, or accepted, on December 15, 1791. They were adopted because some states refused to approve the Constitution unless a Bill of Rights, protecting individuals from various unjust acts of government was added.

Amendment 1

Freedom of religion, speech, and the press;
rights of assembly and petition

Amendment 2

Right to bear arms

Amendment 3

Housing of soldiers

Amendment 4

Search and arrest warrants

Amendment 5

Rights in criminal cases

Amendment 6

Rights to a fair trial

Amendment 7

Rights in civil cases

Amendment 8

Bails, fines, and punishments

Amendment 9

Rights retained by the people

Amendment 10

Powers retained by the states and the people

Amendment 11

Lawsuits against states

Amendment 12

Election of the President and Vice President

Amendment 13

Abolition of slavery

Amendment 14

Civil rights

Amendment 15

African-American suffrage

Amendment 16

Income taxes

Amendment 17

Direct election of senators

Amendment 18

Prohibition of liquor

Amendment 19

Women's suffrage

Amendment 20

Terms of the President and Congress

Amendment 21

Repeal of prohibition

Amendment 22

Presidential term limits

Amendment 23

Suffrage in the District of Columbia

Amendment 24
Poll taxes

Amendment 25
Presidential disability and succesion

Amendment 26
Suffrage for eighteen-year-olds

Amendment 27
Congressional salaries

Chapter Notes

Chapter 1. The Preamble to the United States Constitution

1. Jerome B. Agel, *Words That Make America Great* (New York: Random House, 1997), p. 17.

Chapter 2. Article I: The Legislative Branch

1. Geoffrey R. Stone, Louis M. Seidman, Cass R. Sunstein, and Mark V. Tushnet, *Constitutional Law*, 2nd ed. (Boston: Little, Brown and Company, 1991), p. 838.

Chapter 4. The Powers of Congress

1. Geoffrey R. Stone, Louis M. Seidman, Cass R. Sunstein, and Mark V. Tushnet, *Constitutional Law*, 2nd ed. (Boston: Little, Brown and Company, 1991), p. 142.

2. Eric Foner and John A. Garraty, eds., *The Reader's Companion to American History* (Boston: Houghton Mifflin Company, 1991), pp. 178–179.

3. *Daniel* v. *Paul,* 395 U.S. 298, (1969).

4. *United States* v. *Appalachian Electric Power Co.,* 34 U.S. 377, (1940).

5. *Graham* v. *Richardson,* 403 U.S. 365, (1971).

Chapter 5. Denied Powers

1. *United States* v. *Lovett,* 328 U.S. 303, (1946).

2. *United States* v. *Brown,* 381 U.S. 437, (1965).

3. *Dobbert* v. *Florida,* 432 U.S. 282, (1977).

Chapter 6. Article II: The Executive Branch

1. Presidential Succession Law, 1886

2. "Senate," *World Book Online,* <http://www.worldbook online.com> (June 28, 2001).

3. Ibid

4. *Presidential Oath*

Chapter 7. Powers of the President

1. Commanger, Henry Steele, *Documents of American History,* 8th edition, "Pendleton Act" (Meredith Corporation, 1968), p. 561.

2. Ibid p. 35.

Chapter 8. Article III: The Judicial Branch

1. *Marbury* v. *Madison.*

Glossary

abolitionist—A person who was in favor of doing away with slavery in the United States.

amendment—A revision or addition to a law or to the United States Constitution.

American Woman Suffrage Association (AWSA)—Founded by Lucy Stone, Julia Ward Howe, and Henry Ward Beecher, the AWSA worked for gradual adoption of women's suffrage on a state-by-state basis.

Anti-Federalists—Those who opposed ratifying the Constitution because they feared a strong national government. They included farmers, city workers, and debtors.

bill—A suggested law or proposal that could become law if passed by the House of Representatives and the Senate and signed by the President.

Bill of Rights—The first ten amendments to the United States Constitution. They protect the rights of individuals. The Bill of Rights gives Americans many freedoms and protections such as freedom of religion, speech, and the press.

Centennial Exposition—America's one-hundredth birthday celebration held in Philadelphia during the summer of 1876.

civil trial—A legal action under noncriminal law that seeks to recover damages (in the form of money).

Civil War—The war between the Union (the North) and the Confederacy (the South) from 1861 to 1865.

Congress—Made up of elected representatives in the House and the Senate. It has the power to make the country's laws and raise money for government use.

Connecticut Compromise—The fusion of the Virginia and the New Jersey plans at the Constitutional Convention of 1787. It combined a Senate (made up of two senators per state) with a House of Representatives in which seats were allotted by population.

convention—An assembly called for a specific purpose, such as selecting a candidate for a political office, drafting a constitution, or formulating new policies.

criminal trial—A legal action against someone accused of crimes against the state. Punishments include fines and imprisonment.

Declaration of Independence—Passed in 1776, this document guaranteed freedom for all Americans.

Declaration of Sentiments—A set of resolutions or specific requests passed by the three hundred people attending the Seneca Falls Convention in New York in 1848.

discrimination—Showing prejudice toward a certain group of people, by treating those people differently.

disenfranchise—To deprive someone of the right to vote.

dissent—An opinion written by a Justice who disagrees with the majority of the Court.

double jeopardy—Being tried twice for the same crime. This practice is prohibited by the Fifth Amendment.

due process—Fair and regular procedure provided by law, which is guaranteed to people by the Fifth and Fourteenth Amendments to the Constitution.

eminent domain—The power of the government to take private property for public purposes.

Equal Rights Amendment (ERA)—A proposal to ensure equal pay for men and women for the same jobs, the National Woman's Party began to lobby for another amendment right after the Nineteenth Amendment was passed. The ERA was passed by Congress in 1972, however it was not ratified by the three-quarters of the states required, so the proposal died.

Federalists—A political party organized in 1787 to help achieve ratification of the Constitution. It included planters, merchants, bankers, and manufacturers. They sought a strong central government.

freeholder—A land owner.

grand jury—A group of twelve to twenty-three persons that hears, in private, evidence for serving an indictment.

House of Representatives—One of the two legislative branches of the United States Congress that makes laws.

immunity—A grant of exemption from prosecution in return for a person's testimony. If the person accepts, he or she gives up the right against self-incrimination.

incorporation doctrine—The theory adopted by the Supreme Court since the mid-1930s that applies key parts of the Bill of Rights to the states and the federal government.

Jim Crow laws—Laws that mandated the use of separate facilities for blacks and whites in such public places as restaurants, hotels, barbershops, and railroad cars.

***Miranda* warning**—The caution that police must give criminal suspects in custody, in accord with the Supreme Court's 1966 decision. It warns suspects that they have a right to remain silent, that anything they say can and will be held against them in a court of law, and that they have a right to an attorney.

National American Woman Suffrage Association (NAWSA)—Formed in 1890 with the merging of the National Woman's Suffrage Association and the American Woman Suffrage Association. The group fought for suffrage on both the federal level, by supporting an amendment, and on a state-by-state basis.

National League of Women Voters (NLWV)—Formed by Carrie Chapman Catt as part of the NAWSA in 1919. It became independent a year later. Headquartered in New York City, this organization helps women learn about politics and voting.

National Woman Suffrage Association (NWSA)—A national, pro-suffrage organization that helped fight for the passage of the Nineteenth Amendment. It was created by Elizabeth Cady Stanton and Susan B. Anthony.

National Women's Party (NWP)—Pro-suffrage, national organization formed by Alice Paul. It directed ongoing campaigns against the political party in power, then directly on the president in power, Woodrow Wilson.

New Jersey Plan—The proposal submitted by William Patterson to the Constitutional Convention. It reflected the wishes of small states for equal representation in Congress.

Nineteenth Amendment—Ratified on August 18, 1920, this amendment to the United States Constitution gave women the right to vote in all elections.

nullify—To repeal or remove.

opinion—A written explanation of a judge's decision. It discusses the legal precedents and the reasoning of the court.

poll tax—A fee a person must pay in order to vote.

precedents—Prior legal decisions about an issue currently before a court. The court is expected to decide a case in a way that is consistent with precedent.

primary—An election in which members of a political party select their candidates for office.

property requirement—The stipulation that a person must

own property, usually of at least a certain minimum value, in order to be allowed to vote.

ratification—Giving official approval, passing.

Reconstruction—The period of time after the Civil War that reflected an effort to bring back into the Union the states that had seceded. It also refers to federal efforts to rebuild these states economically and politically.

registrar—An official who signs people up so that they can vote.

resolution—A specific request.

self-incrimination—Providing testimony or evidence against oneself in a criminal trial or investigation. The Fifth Amendment protects a suspect or witness from being forced to testify against himself or herself.

Senate—One of the two legislative branches of the United States Congress that makes laws.

Seneca Falls Convention—The first women's rights convention in the United States, held in Seneca Falls, New York, on July 19-20, 1848.

suffrage—The right to vote.

Supreme Court—The highest court in the United States. It interprets laws and the United States Constitution. The Supreme Court has the power to decide whether a law is constitutional.

Takings Clause—A section of the Fifth Amendment that states that public property may be taken by the government for public use if fair compensation is provided in exchange.

United States Constitution—The highest law of America. This document, which went into effect in 1787, covers the basic laws and principles on which America is governed.

Virginia Plan—The proposal offered by Edmund Randolph at the Constitutional Convention in 1787. It proposed basing representation in Congress on population. This plan was favored by the more populated states.

Woman's Political Union (WPU)—Harriet Stanton Blatch formed this pro-suffrage, national organization in January 1907.

Further Reading

Archer, Jules. They Had a Dream: *The Civil Rights Struggle, From Frederick Douglass to Marcus Garvey to Martin Luther King, and Malcolm X.* New York: Viking Press, 1993.

Bowen, Catherine Drinker. *Miracle at Philadelphia.* Boston: Little Brown and Company, 1966.

Buhle, Mari Jo and Paul, eds. *The Concise History of Woman Suffrage.* Urbana, Ill: University of Illinois Press, 1978.

Dudley, William, ed. *The Creation of the Constitution: Opposing Viewpoints.* San Diego, Calif.: Greenhaven Press Inc., 1995.

Hauptly, Denis J. *A Convention of Delegates—The Creation of the Constitution.* New York: Atheneum, 1987.

Mork, Linda R. *The Bill of Rights: A User's Guide.* Second ed. Close Up Foundation, 1995.

Peltason, J.W. Corwin & Peltason's *Understanding the Constitution.* San Diego, Calif.: Harcourt Brace Jovanovich Publishers, 1991.

Internet Addresses

National Archives and Records Administration, *The Constitution of the United States*
<http://www.archives.gov/exhibit_hall/charters_of_freedom/constitution/constitution.html>

U.S. Constitution – Table of Articles
<http://www.law.cornell.edu/constitution/constitution.overview.html>

Library of Congress, American Memory
<http://memory.loc.gov/const/constquery.html>

Ben's Guide to U.S. Government for Kids, The Constitution
<http://bensguide.gpo.gov/6-8/documents/constitution/index.html>

Index